YOU'RE A WORTHWHILE

PERSON IN MORE WAYS THAN A MILLION!

VALUABLE SERVICES, VALUABLE LIVES:
EVERYDAY PEOPLE MAKING AN EXTRAORDINARY IMPACT

SIMEON W JOHNSON

Printed in the United States of America

Library of Congress Control Number: 2020906740
ISBN: Softcover   978-1-64908-106-3
       eBook   978-1-64376-995-0

Republished by: PageTurner, Press and Media LLC
Publication Date: 05/06/2020

To order copies of this book, contact:

PageTurner Press and Media
Phone: 1-888-447-9651
order@pageturner.us
www.pageturner.us

Dedicated to the
countless women and men who
labor day and night to make
America what it is.

"The society that scorns excellence in plumbing
because plumbing is a humble activity,
and tolerates shoddiness in philosophy because
philosophy is an exalted activity, will have neither
good plumbing nor good philosophy.
Neither its pipes nor its theories will hold water."

John W. Gardner

ACKNOWLEDGEMENTS

I wish to express my deep gratitude to my lovely wife, Dorothy, for her spiritual and moral support in making this project a meaningful endeavor. Without her genuine part- nership and mutual cooperation in everything we do, this book would not have been possible. I am also forever blessed by my two beautiful daughters, Cheryl and Cassandra, who are always such an inspiration to me.

For this book, my major sources of inspiration have been the valiant men and women who go about their jobs day by day, helping others, with incalculable courage and dedica- tion. That is why this book is written—to highlight the essence of your valuable lives as the unsung heroes of everyday life.

In addition, this book would not be what it is today were it not for Judy Katz, my editor, who helped me realize my dream of writing this book. Judy saw the value in these sto- ries, and shepherded this vision from the very beginning. For her editing expertise and meticulous attention to detail, I also extend a heartfelt thanks to Yvonne Koulouthros.

Above all, I thank God, my creator, for giving me this life to live and share with others, and for providing the premise of this book. Most certainly, one individual in particular has been my inspiration. Some 2,000 years ago, a humble carpenter spread the message that God loves us all. In essence, what this holy man conveyed, which has resonated through the ages, is that each and every one of us is worth- while in more ways than a million! In a time of uncertainty and widespread low self-esteem, this message of uncondi- tional love is one that is needed now, more than ever.

PREFACE

Dear Esteemed Reader:

Our species encompasses a giant global family that spans planet earth, and we are all much more alike than we are different. We share the same basic human drives, including the need to survive and feel safe. We all need a sense of belonging in order to live fully and fulfill our creative poten- tial. In order to envision and realize our dreams, however, we need to have confidence in ourselves. Nonetheless, for complex reasons, most people tend to focus more on our differences—how much money we make or don't make, our level of education, our level of skill in the work we do, and how much "stuff" we own—not to mention our differing religious or cultural backgrounds and belief systems. We allow these often-superficial differences to serve as dividing walls between us—or worse, to pit us against one another, separately or as groups or nations. Think of what life might be like if this were not the case!

We also live in a society that worships celebrities, profes- sional athletes, and other often obscenely wealthy people, considering them the "best of the best." With this blind ado- ration and envy of their career successes and, most of all, their privileged, jet-set lifestyles, what we often fail to take into account is the invisible support system enjoyed and taken for granted by these VIPs—and indeed, to some extent, by all of us. Without the critical support of the so- called "little people," their lives, and ours, would quickly come to a grinding halt!

What is this support system? For the privileged few, this might include their agents, accountants, managers, and publicists. It also includes their hairdressers, housekeepers, makeup artists, limo drivers, and others. In this country, 58 percent of the population are engaged in so-called "blue-collar" occupations and subsist on median incomes averaging

$42,000. These unsung and certainly underpaid workers, to me, are as valuable as our society's "stars." After all, when a water pipe bursts, who becomes the most important per- son in your life: a rocket scientist, a mathematician, a brain surgeon— or your plumber?

That's what this book is about—the behind-the-scene peo- ple we tend to overlook, the common men and women who enhance our everyday lives. They deserve our recog- nition and appreciation. They also deserve to value them- selves more than most of them do. Look around—we're everywhere, just doing our jobs with dedication, often going far beyond the expected to keep things moving along smoothly, and to make life more livable and enjoyable for all of us.

In his recent documentary, "Comic," Jerry Seinfeld tells this story: "I was dragging myself back to a comedy club to do my act. I didn't want to do it, just was not in the mood. Then I watched a group of construction workers return to their jobs. Those men were clearly exhausted, the sun was hot. They did not want to go back up thescaffold and do hard physical labor in that hot sun. But they did go back, because it was their job. At that moment I had a revelation. My job is so much easier. If they went back, how could I not?!"

Let's for a moment imagine that we are in a large city when there is a sudden storm, complete with gusty winds and thunderous rains. And let's say that just at that moment, the sanitation workers union goes on strike, and the garbage of 8 million residents goes uncollected. Soon there is pile upon pile of overflowing garbage bags, emitting noxious odors that are going uncollected, graveyards of broken furniture piling up in the streets, and oversized cardboard boxes fill- ing the sidewalks, all thoroughly drenched. At this juncture, what is the value of the sanitation worker—these hard- working people who keep our cities clean? Who would you most want to see on the job that day—the sanitation worker or yet another lawyer or stockbroker?

This rhetorical question once again goes to the heart of this book's contention that all are equal, all play a critical part, and also that we are only as strong as our weakest link. Dr. Martin Luther King, Jr. elegantly expressed this idea when he said: "If a man is called to be a street sweeper, he should sweep the streets even as Michelangelo painted, or Beethoven composed music, or Shakespeare wrote poetry. He should sweep streets so well that all the host of heaven and earth will pause and say, here lived a great street sweeper who did his job well."

Along the same lines, picture what would happen if there were to be the sudden resignation of the entire mainte- nance crew of a high-rise co-op building. Let's throw in mechanical failure—a defective generator, a frozen pipeline, a faulty fuse. Soon, all 600 inhabitants would have no heat or air-conditioning, no running water, no elevator. Soon this co-op's well-heeled shareholders would be rushing down the staircases, pushing and shoving as they run into the street to join the long line outside the one bathroom in the local Starbucks! Others would be in long lines that wrap around the neighborhood stores that are rapidly running out of bottled water and space heaters. Let's add an outside temperature of minus 20 degrees and a heavy snowfall. Where is the building's support staff when you need them? The nerve of those people to want to earn a living wage just for keeping this building operating smoothly!

Consider the Blackout of 2003, which affected all of New York City and its surrounding areas, and extended up into Canada and as far away as the Midwest. We sophisticated human beings in the 21st century take for granted the light bulb and all the other daily necessities that rely on electric- ity. On one extremely hot, muggy day in August, the sce- nario described in the previous paragraph actually took place when the entire Northeast electrical grid in the United States shut down for anywhere from five to 48 hours. Residents of these areas were without air-conditioning or water in their homes. Hoards of people waited in line for water and gas for their cars as well as the opportunity to use a public restroom. Hundreds were stranded for hours in underground subways. When they finally made it home, they huddled next to battery-operated radios in darkness, save for the flickering light from whatever candles they might have had on hand, listening frantically for news as to when their power would return. Still others were stuck in massive traffic jams due to a lack of working traffic lights, with no way to contact their loved ones, since their cell phones were no longer operable.

Hospitals and other such institutions were trying to take care of their patients with the back-up generators they had on hand, some of which failed. Restaurants and grocery stores lost thousands of dollars in spoiled food, and compa- nies whose computers would not turn on lost valuable hours of productivity. As the Mayor of New York City stat- ed on the radio, the only essential employees during the blackout who needed to report to work were those who could fix the actual problems, as well as medical and telecommunications personnel. Everyone else could not get to their jobs—nor were they encouraged to until power was fully restored.

Taking these real circumstances to their logical conclusion is to understand and accept that we humans rely on each other, and that any missing link will break the vital chain. With this reasoning, it is easy to see why every man or woman, no matter what their occupation, is a worthwhile person in more ways than a million.

This book is about, and for, the "working people" and what they—you and I—contribute to daily life, every moment of every day. The individuals profiled in this book are genuine composites of real people working in and around New York City. I am one of those people. Together, our numbers are legion.

We are the backbone, the life force, and the dynamic ener- gy that move the wheels of society forward. The more we respect ourselves, the more others will give us the respect we so richly deserve. Sometimes, however, we are too close to our own lives, too busy doing what we do, to see how important our contributions are to those around us, and to the world at large. This book is my attempt to fill that gap and provide you with the perspective you need to value yourself as richly and completely as you should.

Welcome to my world. And get ready for some surprises!

Contents

"I long to accomplish great and
noble tasks, but it is my chief duty
to accomplish humble tasks as
though they were great and noble.
The world is moved along, not only
by the mighty shoves of its heroes,
but also by the aggregate of the tiny
pushes of each honest worker."

Helen Keller

CHAPTER 1

The Transporters

"Genius is one percent inspiration and 99
percent perspiration."

Thomas Edison

The Airline Baggage Handler

Day in and day out, hundreds of different airplanes take off from John F. Kennedy Airport in Queens, to places far and wide, exotic and ordinary. Airline baggage handler Stan Brown has seen them all—Delta, Aer Lingus, Cathay Pacific, Continental, Kuwaiti Air, Quantas, Aero Mexico. For every flight he's assigned to, there are tens and hun- dreds of passengers, each with their own baggage. For most travelers, the last-minute frenzy of packing and preparing for time away from home makes them want to just "check it all in." Stan knows this, and he takes their prized person- al possessions seriously. He feels that it is his solemn duty and privilege to be entrusted with these travelers' suitcases, animals, strollers, surfboards, appliances, trunks, golf clubs, crates of purchased goods, skis—and all the other various belongings that people pack for a trip.

Outside on the tarmac, Stan braves whatever weather each season brings—torrid heat in the summer, frigid winds and snowstorms in the winter, pelting rain in the spring and fall—and never takes his coal-black eyes off the luggage that passes through his large, calloused hands. His tall, dark muscular frame enables him to lift and load quickly, placing every piece of baggage carefully into the belly of the plane. At the same time, he is attentive to each parcel—in partic- ular the ones that have "FRAGILE" stamped on them in big red letters. Drowning out the deafening sounds of the roar- ing engines that surround him, Stan is also highly focused. He must make sure that each item he loads goes onto the correct flight. The planes' destinations change often enough, so precision is critical to Stan. He always remem- bers to wear his glasses, recommended by his doctor for reading, so that he can easily make out the numbers on the white flight identification labels wrapped around the han- dles of each bag.

Stan's care with each package is further motivated by his own experiences: Two years ago, flying to Dublin to visit his parents, his luggage not only did not arrive till three days later—he later learned that it wound up in Delhi—but it showed up ripped, with half of its contents missing. Then, only six months later, he flew to California to visit an ailing friend, only to discover that his suitcase was sitting in St. Louis instead of Sacramento.

Basically, the way Stan sees it, every bit of stuff packed for a journey is valuable to someone, so it's also important to him. He simply knows all too well that nothing is more satisfying to a weary traveler, standing at the baggage claim terminal, who can't wait to get home and take a shower, than to see the crate containing her beloved, barking golden retriever emerge on the turnstile, soon followed by her favorite maroon suitcase, stuffed to the gills perhaps, but intact! That is why Stan and all the other airline baggage handlers are worthwhile persons in more ways than a million!

The Bus Driver

For bus drivers like Gloria Valez, the souls on board are her sacred responsibility, one she takes seriously. From the moment she slips into her high seat on the Bronx No.10 Crosstown Bus, straps herself in, and adjusts her front and rear view mirrors, she is all eyes and ears, simultaneously alert to the people seated or standing on her bus, waiting at the bus stops, crossing or about to cross the streets. She is also fully aware of the pattern of traffic around her, includ- ing any ambulances, police cars, or fire engines that might change how she drives, which is always defensively.

Anything can, and usually does, happen on her watch: elderly people with canes who board slowly, mothers with strollers, blind people with seeing-eye dogs, noisy kids, people on crutches, and the occasional obstreper- ous drunk. All come with some form of physical or emo- tional "baggage," and Gloria must keep herself focused on her job, on the road, and on the interaction of the lives in her care for as long as they remain on her bus.

The job is long and arduous, with slow traffic and weath- er changes. Snow, sleet, icy conditions, and muggy days pose special challenges, as does the need to stop for people in wheelchairs. Nonetheless, Gloria has been well-trained and, beyond that, is responsible and responsive. She has never missed a day of work, is always cheerful, and keeps her bus on or as close to schedule as possible. Sometimes her patience is sorely tried, like when people ignore the sign that says "Do Not Speak to Driver While Bus is in Motion" and try to engage her in conversation. Gloria understands they are often lonely souls hungry for human dialogue, even with a bus driver. She is always polite, but keeps the conversation short. She has a bigger purpose for being exactly where she is. That is why Gloria and all the other bus drivers are worthwhile persons in more ways than a million!

Did You Know?

Garrett A. Morgan, an African-American, invented the first automatic traffic signal. After witnessing a collision between an automobile and a horse-drawn carriage in the early 1900s, Morgan decided to invent a traffic signal. While others had tested, promoted, and even patented traffic signals, Morgan was one of the first to actually apply for and acquire a U.S. patent for an inexpensive-to-produce traffic signal. The patent was granted in 1923, and Morgan later patented the signal's technology in Great Britain and Canada as well.

The Cab Driver

Zipping around from one end of the city to the other, cab driver Omar Abazz has made it his business, after studying maps long into the night, to know every road in Manhattan, from the long avenues running north and south to the narrow side-streets in the Village. From the moment he puts his key in the ignition of the yellow cab that he is paid to drive at 7:00 a.m. every day, he never stops. Not when he picks up his coffee and Danish to go, nor when he gobbles a hotdog at noon while he studies his "Learn English Instantly" booklet. Nor when he downs Styrofoam cups of coffee throughout the day. He picks up a host of characters: businesspeople, parents and kids, socialites, partygoers (sometimes drunk), actors and actresses. Some have never set foot in a bus or a subway, don't know how to drive, and hate to walk more than five blocks. Omar appreciates his passengers and recognizes that his ride may be their only mode of transportation. He tries to make their ride enjoy- able. That's not always easy when passengers are running late, irritated because of the inevitable traffic jams, or oth- erwise heavily stressed.

Caught in the thick of rush hour, with cars maneuvering precariously close to one another as an ambulance's siren sounds nearby, passengers have often thrown money at Omar and hastily run out. Others have even vomited in the back and made no effort to clean up their mess. Two guys tried to mug him recently, prompting his boss to install a bulletproof glass divider. The divider prevents him from chatting as much with his riders to practice his English, but he still makes an effort to be friendly.

Omar doesn't experience as much prejudice as he did when he arrived in the United States from Pakistan two years ago. There is still an occasional bigot, though. Omar acts as though he has not heard the slur as he artfully weaves in and out of traffic, watching for jay-walking pedestrians, the never-ending road construction areas, vehicles that brake abruptly, and horse-drawn carriages. Whether he receives a tip or not, Omar says "Thank you" to the departing passen- ger, grateful he can earn a living to support his wife, son, and twin daughters, as well as send money back to his homeland to feed and clothe the large extended family that depends on him.

When he finally returns home, exhausted, to his small apartment in Queens, usually well after dark, his wife often has her coat on with their kids dressed to go out. They have to go to the grocery store, or some other impor- tant destination, she invariably reports. Omar wishes his wife knew how to drive! Like most cab drivers, Omar takes his job seriously, safely transporting people to and fro in the city that never sleeps. That is why Omar and all the other cab drivers are worthwhile persons in more ways than a million!

The Truck Driver

It's another lonely, rainy night for truck driver Terry McCurran. He pulls into the deserted rest stop just past Exit 9 off the New York State Thruway and parks his royal blue 18-wheeler. He looks around the parking lot. Seems safe, he thinks. You can never be too sure after the murder and rob- bery of that trucker in Connecticut, the one who was attacked while he slept at a rest stop, in his truck in broad daylight. Terry looks at his clock—12:10 a.m. He started his trek some 12 hours ago, when the temperature reached 34 degrees and finally thawed out the roads. Now, with dark- ness enveloping him like a wool cloak, Terry has trouble keeping his eyes open, despite the freezing air his open window brings in and the bright lights of the other gigantic trucks that speedily pass by him on the highway. He real- izes that he should have stopped to nap a few hours ago, but the traffic was so miserable that he lost time. And he has to get to the Canadian border before sunrise. He can not risk spoiling his truck's cargo, perishable items such as dairy products, eggs, fruits, and vegetables.

Running his gnarled hands through his graying thick black hair, Terry reasons that he has to get at least a few hours of sleep. His thoughts are interrupted by the CB radio. His supervisor's booming voice comes through loud and clear: "Terry, where in the world have ya been?

I have not heard from you since three! Ten-four." Terry hastily picks up the receiver to the CB: "Sorry, boss, but I got caught in some bumper-to-bumper 'cause of a four- car accident. I was gonna call ya after I made up the time and pulled over, which I just did. I should get to the bor- der on time, as long as it doesn't start snowing. Forecast sounds better. Ten-four."

His boss responds with a short grunt and then a click. Just as Terry begins to close his hazel eyes, another voice greets him: "Hi, sugar-pie-sweetie, it's me. Where are ya? Ten- four." It's his wife, Nancy. "Hey there, lady-love," Terry replies. "How are you and my baby boy? Ten-four." Nancy fills him in on the home life back in Coney Island, while Terry pulls out half of the hamburger that he left in his truck from yesterday. It's going to be a long night, he realizes, as he leans back in his worn vinyl seat and stretches his sore legs. He still has to log all his hours and do a bunch of paperwork before he reaches Canada, he suddenly remem- bers. With Nancy still chattering away in the background, he opens a can of Coke, silently praying that the caffeine will give him a boost. If only his trucker buddy Dave could have come along to split the driving, but now with the recent spate of layoffs.... Terry wasn't looking forward to the drive back down either, but the return shipment was due in Florida in 80 hours. No rest for the weary, he thinks, sighing. And that is why Terry and all the other truck driv- ers are worthwhile persons in more ways than a million!

Remember also the:

- pilot
- subway operator
- train conductor

- and all the transporters!

They are each worthwhile persons in more ways than a million!

"Everything that is really great and
inspiring is created by the individual
who can labor in freedom."

Albert Einstein

CHAPTER 2

The Machines Around Us

"While we have the gift of life, it seems to
me the only tragedy is to allow part of us to
die — whether it is our spirit, our creativity,
or our glorious uniqueness."

Gilda Radner

The Electrician

Every morning, right before the sun rises, electrician Kolya Jackowski leaves his two-family home in Brooklyn. He rarely knows what his entire day will bring. He has regular jobs at various office complexes throughout Brooklyn and Staten Island; their heaters and air-conditioners have to be frequently checked and maintained. The rest of Kolya's cus- tomers, who are mostly cultivated through word of mouth, however, run the gamut from suburbanites in Long Island and wealthy couples on Manhattan's Upper East Side, to low-income families in the Bronx and yuppies in Hoboken.

At any given moment, even in the middle of the night, one or more of these customers will call him on his cell phone, panicked and demanding. He then hops into his 10-year-old faded blue Chevy van and makes his way to wherever the crisis is taking place. On this particular morning, he is on his way to East 85th Street and York Avenue, where Mr. and Mrs. Lexington, the 40-something owners of a five-story multimillion-dollar penthouse, are waiting. Just two days ago, he wired an extensive surround-sound stereo for their

home theater. It broke down an hour ago, they frantically relay. "Oh, and Kilya, please come over here too," com- mands the heavily made-up wife (why can she never get my name right, Kolya wonders?) with a wave of her mani- cured, bejeweled hand. "You see the light bulb that's out up there above the kitchen sink? Neither Clark nor I can get up there, so we left it up there for you to change."

Kolya obediently climbs up the small stepladder he brought along, changes the bulb, and then moves on to the stereo. It turns out that their outdated intercom system, which they hardly use, had blown a fuse, causing the stereo to go haywire. Kolya sees the faulty fuse clearly and repairs the stereo system. Just as Kolya climbs into his van after fixing the problems at the penthouse, his wife's cousin Teresa in the South Bronx calls him. He barely recognizes her voice, she is that agitated. Their refrigerator just died, she exclaims, and they are having all of her husband's 20 relatives over for her father-in-law's birthday tomorrow night! Could Kolya come right away to repair it? She cannot afford to have the 15 pounds of sausage, chicken, and beef go bad! Kolya says he's on his way. As he heads onto the Harlem River Drive, his wife calls. Please come home, she begs. No heat is coming out of the furnace, and their three teenage daughters and newborn son are shivering, huddled around the sole working heater in his parents' bed- room downstairs. Kolya glances at his watch. He'll have to make a quick detour home before heading to the Bronx. Human beings rely too much on machines, Kolya mutters to himself, especially ones that run only on electricity. Yes we do. And that is exactly why Kolya and all the other electri- cians are worthwhile persons in more ways than a million!

Did You Know?

In 1940, African-American Fredrick McKinley Jones received a patent for his invention of an automatic refrigeration system—a roof-mounted cooling device—for long-haul trucks. Jones was the first person to invent a practical, mechanical refrigeration system for trucks and railroad cars. This, in turn, eliminated the risk of food spoilage during long-distance shipping trips. The system was subsequently adapted to a variety of other common carriers, including ships.

The Elevator Technician

The alarm from several floors above causes elevator technician Manny Klekos to jerk his head and look up. "Oh no," he mumbles, as he stands in the freight eleva- tor he's been trying to repair. "Don't tell me someone is stuck again," he moans to himself.... Sure enough, Pete, the doorman of the posh midtown-Manhattan 15-story office building he's been working in, comes rushing over, panting. "Manny, Manny," he says, "the Mayor is stuck in between the 10th and 11th floors. His aides say he is highly claustro- phobic and could start to hyperventilate at any time!"

"Oh, boy," Manny thinks to himself. "I'll be right there," he says to Pete, as he collects his tools and leaps up the stairs to the 10th floor. At least there is no fire. He has not been able to work around any smell of smoke since 9/11, when he tried to fix one of the jammed elevators in the World Trade Center. He narrowly escaped himself and will never forget the screams of those trapped inside. At least once a month his fire-engulfed dreams bring him back to that horrendous day. But today he must—and will—save the Mayor. As he reaches the 10th floor, he sees that the Mayor's bodyguards have been trying to jimmy the top of the elevator's door. Manny asks them to step aside and also asks if they have been able to communicate with the Mayor and whoever else is stuck with him. Yes, they say, they were able to reach the Mayor's deputy on his cell phone. He and the Mayor are the only ones in the elevator.

Manny asks them to dial the deputy's number. He then gets on the phone and instructs the deputy to open the emergency box and turn the red knob to the left. After this step, Manny pries the elevator's door open with his large pliers, climbs on top of the elevator, and begins to examine its wiring and cables. An area of only six square feet sur- rounds him. Manny also tries to keep his deep brown eyes from straying downward; since 9/11, he has been combat- ing a fear of heights, especially when he feels pressured— as he does now. In just a few minutes, however, he finds the foot-long faulty cable and replaces it with one of the spares in his toolbox. Then he jumps off the elevator, his wavy black hair shooting straight up, and calls the deputy again to give him instructions.

Moments later, on the 11th floor, the elevator, with the Mayor and his deputy in tow, arrives. Both men are alert

but visibly shaken. The bodyguards waste no time whisk-ing them away, just as Manny's supervisor John calls him, asking why the freight elevator is still stuck in the sub-base-ment of the building. "The guys on the 7th floor need their computers now from that floor! They've been waiting for four hours, since 9:00 a.m.!" John practically yells.

"OK, I'm on it," Manny replies quietly, unhooking the top button of his sepia-colored uniform. He wishes that his dad, one of the first second-generation elevator technicians, had warned him about John. Well, for now this job is okay, Manny thinks, but if I ever want to get married and have kids, maybe it would be better to work in a less stressful set- ting, like at Uncle Mike's diner, right near my apartment in Astoria. On the other hand, Manny concludes, there's noth- ing like the satisfaction of fixing a mode of fickle transporta- tion like an elevator. People depend on it to get where they need to go, quickly. And that is why Manny, his father and grandfather before him, and all the other elevator techni- cians, are worthwhile persons in more ways than a million!

Did You Know?

African-American Alexander Miles patented an electric eleva- tor in 1887. While Miles did not invent the first elevator, he improved the method of the opening and closing of elevator doors. In addition, Miles created an automatic mechanism that closed access to the shaft. This was a very welcome invention, because in the late 1800s, elevator patrons or oper- ators were often required to manually shut a door to cut off access to the elevator shaft. People would forget to close the shaft door, and accidents would then occur when people fell down elevator shafts.

The Mechanic

On her way back from the local junkyard with a spare tire under her arm, mechanic Kathy Moore stops to buy a cup of coffee for her 3:00 p.m. caffeine boost. She's been up since 6:00 a.m. and at work—Hank's Autobody Shop in Brooklyn Heights, right down the street from her apart- ment—since 7:30 that morning after dropping her son Randy off at school. It never fails that another mom, upon seeing golden-haired Kathy in a mechanic's uniform, will look at her with a surprised gaze. So what if she's the only woman at the shop, Kathy thinks. She had grown up around cars, with her dad and uncle always fixing them up, and her mom likewise mechanically inclined....

Back at Hank's, she ducks into the warehouse to see if the engine piece for the pesky Jaguar has come in yet. No such luck. Well, she'll just get to working on the transmission and the distributor in the Cadillac, fix the air-conditioner in the Bronco, and then change the tire on the Honda with the one she just found. As Kathy finishes her cup of cof- fee, she nearly collides with Hank, the shop's owner, who supposedly retired right before Kathy started. She had heard about Hank's harassing tendencies and would not have taken the job if he was still there. Hank's son Cliff is the complete opposite, respectful and polite, but Hank can't resist making degrading remarks and lewd gestures to her. So Kathy quickly ducks out of Hank's way. "Hey, woman, I've got something for you," Hank says teasingly. Kathy turns her head, gives Hank a piercing look with her dark green eyes, then notices the Jaguar piece in Hank's hands. "What'ya gonna give me for it?" he taunts.

Used to Hank's games, Kathy walks away and opens the hood to the Cadillac. What a mess, she thinks, looking closely. This problem with the transmission itself could take a whole day to fix. She rolls up her sleeves, grabs a wrench, and ignores Hank, who hovers around her. "Don't you want this?" he prods. Kathy turns around and slides herself under the Bronco, so Hank can't be lit- erally in her face. Well, at least this Bronco's AC problem won't take too long to remedy. Randy's school will be letting out in 45 minutes, so she can pick him up after she finishes the Bronco and then come back to deal with the Caddy. Oh, and the Honda too. "I guess the Jaguar will have to wait till tomorrow," she says out loud. Those foreign cars are such a pain sometimes—when their parts are defective, it takes forever to get replace- ments, and then who knows how long Hank will hang onto it. But that's what happens when you're a woman in a man's world, she thinks, sighing. It's not easy being a single mom either, but at least Randy can hang out here after school while I get these cars going, Kathy reflects. Anyhow, there's no way Hank is going to push me out, Kathy resolves. Cliff knows I'm one of the best mechan- ics around and that I'll work however long it takes to get a job done, not to mention scour the junkyard for inex- pensive parts. It's precisely this tenacity, resourcefulness and skill that make Kathy and all the other mechanics worthwhile persons in more ways than a million!

Did You Know?

In 1932, African-American Richard Spikes patented an improved automatic gear shift, so that the gears for the various speeds were in constant mesh. Spikes invented a clutch mechanism for his shift, using levers to shift gears.

Remember also the:

- cable installer
- gas meter reader
- heavy equipment operator and all those who manage the machines around us!

They are each worthwhile persons in more ways than a million!

"No race can prosper until it
learns there is as much dignity in
tilling a field as in writing a poem."

Booker T. Washington

CHAPTER 3

Building, Digging & Shaping

"...You must prepare the ground, plant the seed, cultivate, and water if you expect to reap the harvest."

Stephen B. Covey

The Bricklayer

As the sun rises at 6:30 a.m. on another summertime Saturday, bricklayer Clarence Jeffers starts his workday. Today he has been assigned to a $3.2-million mansion in the suburbs of Basking Ridge, New Jersey. The owners, a middle-aged wife and her practically non-participatory older husband, hired him to do the painstaking work of lay- ing one brick at a time for their castle-like home, whose exterior is to be a combination of the off-white and tan-col- ored bricks which were imported straight from Italy.

With his pile of Italian bricks and big bucket of gray mortar, Clarence begins his bricklaying routine of stirring the mortar a couple of times swiftly before placing each brick. The mortar must be the right consistency and also the right temperature; if the sun is too strong, the mortar may dry out. So he must work quickly. He can lay and layer about 20 bricks a minute, a pretty good time, but when he has a job like this—a total of 1,000 bricks for the front exterior alone—his work is cut out for him, especially since the temperature is already 87 degrees. Clarence prefers to work in autumn, when the weather is cooler and not as rainy or snowy. But these wealthy customers tend to do their renovations in the summer, it seems, and Clarence cannot say no if he wants to retire anytime soon. So, with his big bucket of mortar and shiny spade, he makes his way carefully up the scaffolding he must ascend, eventually all the way to the top floor, three sto- ries above ground.

By noon, the sun is out in full force, and the humidity makes it feel even hotter. Sweat drips from Clarence's graying hair, as he wipes his tan forehead with the red bandana he keeps stuffed in the back pocket of his blue jean overalls. In another hour he probably will have to take his tank top off, he thinks. Otherwise, he'll be soaked with perspiration. He grows uncomfortable at the prospect of the demanding wife, who peers at him lasciv- iously, especially when he has taken off his shirt. Unfortunately, as he must start bricklaying from the bot- tom up, he often winds up on the top floor—where her bedroom is—when the temperature has reached its all-time daily high and he needs to disrobe even a little just to continue his efficient pace. The lady of the house seems to always purposely plant herself on her cavernous king- sized bed, with its shiny lavender sheets. She is decked out in lacy black lingerie and licks her lips. Clarence has asked his boss to send him elsewhere, but to no avail. His boss just snickers whenever he relays his discomfort. "You should be so lucky," he sneers at Clarence. "Plus, Mrs. Anderson is one of our most reliable customers, and she requested you."

Clarence feels caught between a brick and a hard place. Even mentioning his sweet wife Melissa and their four grown children does not seem to deter the mistress of this monstrosity at 15 McDougal Lane. He thinks that it might be time to call Dave, his neighbor in Bay Ridge, who owns a corporate construction company, to see if he can get out of this residential line of work. The money may be good, but the customers can make his days too trying. He's afraid that if he turns Mrs. Anderson down again, she will have him fired anyway. In the meantime, he keeps plodding away—ivory brick, mortar, tan brick, mortar, ivory brick again, and on and on. This unquestionable dedication and expertise is precisely why Clarence and all the other brick- layers are worthwhile persons in more ways than a million!

The Carpenter

Drake Higgins makes his way into his workshop, where the smell of freshly cut wood awaits him. In his 20 years as a carpenter, that aroma never fails to stimulate him to eagerly begin working. On this particular morning, howev- er, he decides to first take a walk in his Staten Island neigh- borhood to think about how he is going to make the spe- cial-order dresser for his newest customer. It will be about seven feet high and six feet wide, with about 15 drawers and 10 shelves. What Drake looks forward to the most is crafting the dresser's legs. He thinks he will go for the elegant classic look, like that Louis XVI-type furniture, but without the gilded finish. This dresser will be made of the finest mahogany, which costs a pretty penny. But at least he can get it for cost, so he can give this customer, a middle- aged gentleman named Howard, a nice deal. Howard said that if this piece turns out well, he will have more for Drake to create. Sounds like Howard may be getting married, Drake guesses, and that this dresser is to be an old-fash- ioned engagement present of sorts.

Once downstairs in the basement—his workshop—Drake puts his protective glasses over his light brown eyes and red hair and turns on his woodcutting machine, but not before checking that the safety latch is on properly. Just a few months ago he lost a bit of his left pinky when he was not careful. Sawdust starts to fly around as Drake slices the first of 10 pieces of thick wood. Glancing at the clock, he real- izes that he still has an appointment at noon for yet anoth- er cabinetry job in New Jersey. He would rather stay in his workshop, but he needs the extra money to pay for the addition—a nursery for the baby that's on the way—that he and his wife Sarah want to build onto their small yellow Cape Cod-style house.

The phone rings. It's Camille Perry, one of his customers from Manhattan. She asks him if he can come over tonight, once her husband is home. They found something not quite right with the bar he created for them. Drake sighs and says he has to check and will call her back. That was one of his most time-consuming jobs, a bar the length of one entire 15-foot wall. The wood was not taking that well to the varnish, but Drake could not tell what the end result would be until it fully dried, which probably happened yes- terday. He had warned the Perrys about his concerns, but they weren't worried, they said. They just wanted this bar made out of the wood they brought back from Maine. That's the problem with transporting some kinds of wood yourself, Drake thinks, as he goes upstairs to look at Sarah's calendar. You never know how it will travel or breathe in a different environment. He picks up the phone and dials. "Hi, Mrs. Perry, it's Drake. Looks all clear for me to come by at seven tonight. Okay, see you then."

Drake returns to his workshop and picks up a shaver. Then he starts whittling away at the mahogany wood he just cut. Well, at least I have most of today to start the dresser, he says to himself, smiling. You can't beat creating something of lasting beauty with nature's magnificent resources and your own hands, he thinks. That's simply why Drake and all the other carpenters are worthwhile persons in more ways than a million!

The Farmer

Every morning without fail, no matter what day of the week or what season it is, the rooster's crow at 5:00 a.m. wakes Matilda Gibbons, a farmer in Montauk, Long Island. She rolls out of bed and throws a red flannel shirt over her tousled silver-blond hair before climbing into a pair of worn beige overalls. Time to feed the chickens, she says to her- self, mantra-like, then milk the cows, plow the wheat fields, and prune the grapes in the vineyards. How she wishes her husband Jack was here, but years of toil took its toll on him, so much so that he died from a heart attack last year. Now, Matilda has to run their farm, Whipper-Snapper Grove, on her own. Well, she's grateful for her two hired hands, Charlie and Frank. Too bad she never had any chil- dren to help out with the land.

After quickly downing a cup of black coffee and a banana bran muffin from the batch of 20 she made yesterday, Matilda steps outside. Looks like a nice day, she thinks, her hazel eyes fixed on the powder-blue sky filled with puffy white clouds.

Early fall is such a nice time of year, she reflects, as she looks out at the 60 acres that comprise domain. She pauses to sit for a moment on the cherry rock- ing chair on her farmhouse's front porch, thinking of the other daily tasks that she, with Charlie and Frank, must accomplish today: feed the two dogs, four cats, and three horses; clean all the rugs in the house; stack the hay in the small barn; wash the dogs; clean out the big barn; assemble the eggs for delivery; groom the horses and finish building the fence around the vineyard. Maybe, if she has time, she'll ride Sugar, her favorite horse, to the beach a mile away, for a breather. Nothing like hearing the ocean waves after a hectic workday, she muses.

Matilda looks at her watch: 5:40 a.m. In less than three hours the delivery boy will be here to pick up the eggs from her 25 chickens. Should be a good bunch, she calculates, so she might break even this month. The milk from her 15 cows, on the other hand, is not so promising. Well, she has till next week to see how much they can produce before that egg pick-up takes place. At least the wheat looks profitable this year— definitely not like last year, given the drought, fol- lowed by a fire, that ruined more than half of her crop. "I hope this winter is milder," Matilda wishes out loud, rubbing her calloused, wrinkled hands. Last year, the unprecedented amounts of ice and snow wiped out her entire vineyard. Granted, it was the first year that she undertook that endeav- or, with hopes of a more profitable income overall, but it was disappointing nonetheless. So many hours she had spent, in humid sunshine and cold darkness, planting those grape vines. Well, maybe in five years they will have some bottles of Chardonnay to show for it. In the meantime, it's getting late, she realizes. The chickens are waiting, as are all the other chores piling up around the farm. And she just remem- bered how she wants to start sanding and staining all the hard-wood floors in her house! This endless perseverance and industriousness is exactly why Matilda and all the other farmers are worthwhile persons in more ways than a million!

Remember also the:

- blacksmith
- miner
- silversmith
- steelworker
- stonecutter
- welder and all those who build, dig, and shape!

They are each worthwhile persons in more ways than a million!

"Don't be afraid to give your best
to what seemingly are small jobs.
Every time you conquer one, it
makes you that much stronger.
If you do the little jobs well, the
big ones will tend to take care of
themselves."

Dale Carnegie

CHAPTER 4

Cleanliness Counts

"If a man is called to be a street sweeper, he
should sweep streets even as Michelangelo
painted, or Beethoven composed music, or
Shakespeare wrote poetry."

Martin Luther King, Jr.

The Dishwasher

It's noon on a Friday, and dishwasher Carlos Perez is starting his long weekend shift. He left his home in the Bronx two hours before to get on a bus, and then another, that take him to the suburbs of New Jersey, in Cedar Grove. There, at the 300-seat La Familia Ristorante, with its gilded doors and red velvet-covered chairs, is where Carlos works six days a week, washing dishes for over 12 hours straight.

Though La Familia has a few heavy-duty dishwashers, the restaurant still depends on workers like Carlos to scrape off each plate and piece of silverware, usually laden with pasta, sticky sauces made of cheese or tomatoes, meats, and nearly every type of high-priced Italian meal imaginable. He has to make sure that all the morsels of food are neatly disposed of before rinsing each piece of china or cutlery with steaming hot, sudsy water and placing it carefully in the deep dishwasher. Carlos tries to be careful to not let the plates slip from his hand, but inevitably one will fall out of his fingers and break on the floor.

It's worse when the restaurant's owner, Roberto, is around. He tends to yell at Carlos and Juan, the other dishwasher who shares his shift. But after three years of washing La Familia's flatware, Carlos has gotten his dishwashing routine down to a science: scrap, lather, rinse, and into the dishwasher it goes.

With glasses, while there's no scraping involved, the chance of breakage is higher, so Carlos tends to take off his thick yellow rubber gloves while washing glasses. His small hands, red and swollen from their time spent under hot running water, move quickly as he washes the wine glasses, tumblers, cups, brandy snifters, and all the other drinking devices from which the restaurant's patrons con- sume their liquids. He keeps his soft brown eyes on the breakables that pass through his hands, and this focus usually prevents any damage. But he can barely take a break, except to use the bathroom. Otherwise he risks being yelled at by Roberto, who tends to lurk around in the kitchen.

At well past midnight, when he wraps up his shift, Carlos just wants to take off his red-and-white checkered apron and sit down. And sit he does, on his two-hour bus ride back to his two-bedroom apartment in the Bronx. When he arrives home, his three cousins from Mexico are already sleeping soundly. After taking off his sneakers, jeans, and T-shirt and changing into his sweats, Carlos usually likes to watch a little TV in their tiny kitchen before washing his curly black hair and going to bed. During commercials he'll count his money (he's happy to receive all cash) and set aside the amount he sends weekly to his parents and siblings in Mexico. This diligence and tenacity are why Carlos and all the other dishwashers are worthwhile persons in more ways than a million!

The Janitor

The alarm rings at 5:00 a.m., and janitor Michael Harrison promptly swings his large legs out of bed, kisses Jane, his wife of 30 years, on the cheek, and makes his way to the bathroom. He has exactly 45 minutes to be at work at the elementary school down the block in his Staten Island neighborhood. By 5:45 a.m. he is opening the doors of Clark School, just 75 minutes before 300 children will enter the big red-brick building.

His first order of the day is to make sure that all the lights go on and that everything is up and running. He enjoys this quiet time, as he strolls though the many hallways and classrooms and offices. Then he starts making rounds with all the cleaning supplies that he keeps well-stocked in his small janitor's closet. It's this early time in his day that Michael appreciates the most. When the kids start coming, that's when things get loud and messy.

In his navy blue jumpsuit, Michael is easily recognizable to the schoolchildren. Some smile and call his name, while others—the bullies especially—make mean comments, whether it's about his weight, his dark skin, or whatever.

The principal of the school, Mrs. Hoffman, has asked Michael to bring these misbehaving kids to her attention, so he does, though reluctantly. Michael would rather just get along with everybody. Usually, he does. The teachers treat him well and are grateful that they will walk into clean class- rooms every morning, thanks to his care and attention.

Throughout the day Michael takes care of odds and ends and spills and leaks, whether in the boiler room, the gym, the cafeteria, or elsewhere. But his day really starts to get busy around 2:30 p.m., when the kids begin boarding the buses to go home. Then it's time to hustle. Into each of the 30 classrooms he goes, picking up the garbage, vacuuming and mopping the floors, wiping the fingerprints off the win- dows, and more. Then it's time to check out the restrooms, often a disaster area—toilet paper, drops of urine, paper towels, trails of liquid soap, lipstick smudges on the mir- rors, remnants of crumbled eye shadow, even sanitary nap- kins (those sixth graders are growing up too fast these days, he thinks!), and whatever else the kids decide to leave behind in the restrooms (like a test with a "D" on it).

One restroom can take as long as five classrooms for Michael to clean, and an overflowing toilet can make the process even longer. Michael also tidies up the administra- tion offices before locking up and heading to the one-story brownstone he and Jane have lived in for the past 25 years. On his walk home, he starts to think about when he wants to retire. Maybe in two years or so, he muses. Then I will be eligible to receive my pension, and we can move to Florida and be near the grandkids. In the meantime though, he's still got a large school to maintain. This is why Michael and all the other janitors are worthwhile persons in more ways than a million!

Did You Know?

George T. Sampson, an African-American, received a patent for the clothes dryer in 1892.

A year later, African-American Thomas Stewart patented a new type of mop—one that could wring the water out of itself by the use of a lever.

The Window Washer

It's a clear day full of sunshine at 8:00 a.m., when window washer Oscar Reggia leaves his studio in Jersey City on his way to work. Today he'll be at a 50-story high-rise in lower Manhattan. Driving his company's white van, with the words "Willie's Window Washing" emblazoned on it in big red and blue letters, Oscar listens to the weather forecast—going to reach 90 degrees, possibly a record for the month of May— while making his way to the job site.

After spending nearly a half hour to find a spot (his boss hates to pay for parking), Oscar unloads the van: harness, bucket, squeegee, and window cleaning solution. He almost forgets his sunglasses—so necessary on a sunny day, when high in the sky without them, the sun's rays can pierce his light green eyes so much that they hurt.

After passing through security in the lobby of the high-rise, Oscar takes the elevator to the top floor and asks for the super, Mr. Jacobs. A good half hour passes before the man comes out. By this time, Oscar has figured out where to start washing the 11-foot windows. If he starts on the east side, he figures, the sun won't be shining on him when he gets to the west side. When Mr. Jacobs finally appears, he acknowledges Oscar with a grunt and leads him to the open-air passageway that enables him to access the win- dows. Once Mr. Jacobs sees that Oscar knows what he is doing, he abruptly leaves. Oscar prefers it that way. There is nothing worse, he thinks, as he straps the harness around his body, than being scrutinized by someone while dan- gling 50 stories up in the air!

31

Making sure that the harness is securely fastened around his torso and bottom, Oscar next fills the bucket with the cleaning solution and dunks the squeegee in the liquid. He then carefully clamps the harness's hook on to the appropriate lever on the window frame. Holding the bucket in one hand and the squeegee in the other, Oscar makes his way to the end of the passageway and slowly sits down on the edge, making sure not to look down. Though he does not have a fear of heights, Oscar is never quite sure how he'll feel if he looks down, and chooses to not take chances. Adjusting the rope on the harness to make sure he has enough slack, Oscar slowly moves his body away from the ledge he was sitting on. Soon he is sitting fully in the harness, supported only by the safety hook that keeps him attached to the building. He is about a foot away from the windows. By maneuvering his body in his swift, skilled fashion, he is able to pick up the bucket and squeegee he left on the ledge and begin his job with the first of 500 win- dows. If the weather holds out till 7:00 p.m., he should be able to finish a quarter of his job today, Oscar figures. He begins his methodical process: dip squeegee into bucket, apply squeegee to window and streak it down, reverse squeegee and dry window. With 10 strokes, he is done with the first window on the 50th floor. He proceeds to the next, keeping his focus on his surroundings, not—as some of his male co-workers do—on the individuals (particularly the attractive businesswomen) and goings-on inside. It is pre- cisely this concentration, attention to detail, and discretion that make Oscar and all the other window washers worth- while persons in more ways than a million!

Remember also the:

- busboy and busgirl
- carpet cleaner
- car washer
- cleaning person
- street sweeper and all those for whom cleanliness counts!

They are each worthwhile persons in more ways than a million!

"Every calling is great when greatly
pursued."

Oliver Wendell Holmes

CHAPTER 5

The Image-Enhancers

"Work is love made visible."

Khalil Gibran, *The Prophet*

The Drycleaner

The bell on Chung Li's drycleaner shop door rings repeatedly as the customers come strolling in, one after the other, their arms loaded down with shirts, suits, skirts, and what- ever else they need to be professionally laundered. In her 25 years of owning this dry-cleaning business in Long Island with her husband Jee, never has Chung seen it so busy as it has been this past year. It must be the new condominium complex they built a few blocks away, Chung thinks. Maybe we should have bought a unit, she further rumi- nates, but then we probably would not be able to afford going to see our parents in Korea every year. Or flying them to Chung and Jee's home, an apartment just above their shop. Not to mention paying for some of their medical bills. And as it is, it's hard enough saving for their sole child's col- lege education. At least Sung Yi, their daughter, helps out at the store. Between her and her cousin Tina, Chung has not felt the need to hire anyone else. But she may have to, after Sung Yi leaves for college. Chung quickly tags each cus- tomer's article of clothing, logs it into the computer with their phone number, and hands them their receipt.

Thankfully, receiving clothes is a faster process than finding them on the long motorized rack. The worst is when one of the upper-crust women from the neighboring town finds something to complain about as they receive their clothes. "I asked for heavy starch, not medium," one will often say, even though the slip says "medium" and Tina had wit- nessed the woman saying as much to her mother. Chung will always comply with the customer—as her own moth- er used to say, "The customer is always right." Perhaps it's this attitude that makes her shop so popular. But on a hot summer day, when the steam in the back of the shop reach- es an all-time high of over 100 degrees, Chung has to step aside and take a breath after dealing with an irate customer. Too much heat, she feels. The four of them work quickly. If only some of the clientele knew how much they accom- plished in their 14-hour days, 6 days a week. To clean, iron, and keep track of nearly 1,000 pieces of clothing every week is no small feat, as Chung knows all too well.

On this particular Saturday, easily the busiest day of the week, with at least 75 customers a day, Chung focuses on the digital clock on her cash register as she gives her cus- tomers change. Only five more hours to go before closing the doors, cleaning the store, counting the money, check- ing all the machines and supplies, reconciling the comput- er systems, and stopping by the bank. Then it's time to go home, upstairs. As convenient as their commute to work is, it's sometimes hard to take a break from it all. Inevitably, Chung will remember some piece of paper- work she has yet to fill out, and down the stairs of her apartment she'll go, into the shop, sometimes at 2:00 a.m., to take care of unfinished business; otherwise, she cannot sleep. This dedication and service is what makes Chung and all the other drycleaners worthwhile persons in more ways than a million!

Did You Know?

African-American Sarah Boone patented an improvement to the ironing board in 1892. Boone's ironing board, designed to be effective in ironing the sleeves and bodies of ladies' garments, was very narrow and curved, the size and fit of a sleeve. It was also reversible, making it easy to iron both sides of a sleeve.

The Hairdresser

Her piercing periwinkle eyes peering out of the small win- dow in her cramped salon, hairdresser Liliya Rachnov spots her first customer, right on time at 9:00 a.m. She knows how grateful her customers are for her salon, the only one in this part of Queens that's open on Sundays. Liliya makes the effort to keep them loyal—her homemade chocolate donuts and freshly brewed French Vanilla coffee always put smiles on their faces.

"Hi, Clarice," Liliya says with a smile to the large, elderly red-haired woman opening the door emblazoned with "Lovely Liliya's" in pink curlique script. "Help yourself to some coffee and a donut," Liliya continues. "I'll be right with you. I'm just finishing up preparing your color." Clarice complies with a hungry look in her eye, and Liliya quickly grabs the hair products and the tools she uses to enhance Clarice's thinning hair. She helps Clarice to the chair and elevates it slowly, asking Clarice about her newest grandchild and the rest of her news.

While chattering away and combing the tangles out of Clarice's ruby tresses, Liliya eyes the clock, hoping that Daniella and Tanya make it in soon—they're expecting three more customers at 9:30 a.m., all with hair appoint- ments and then manicures and pedicures with Anna, who comes in at 10:30 a.m. It promises to be a full day, with customers straight through until closing at 7:00 p.m. Thank goodness tomorrow is her one day off, Liliya sighs, as she runs her fingers through her own wavy blond hair. The salon needs a thorough cleaning. No matter how much nightly clean-up that they do, it never seems to be enough. And she has to do her bills, take inventory of all her supplies, place whatever orders, and finish the new advertising materials she's working on with her neighbor, who's a designer. Then late tomorrow afternoon she has to take her twin teenage sons to the professional basket- ball game she promised them. Why must Sergey be away on yet another business trip to Russia, she mutters to her- self, a frown creeping onto her otherwise smooth ivory forehead, as she thinks of her often absent husband. Well at least he got us the basketball tickets for free. They cer- tainly could not have afforded them.

Like clockwork, her next three customers file in, followed by an out-of-breath Daniella. "Good morning," all four say in unison, as all but Daniella make their way towards Liliya's donuts. A tired-looking Tanya walks in next, and soon the small salon is humming with activity. The day goes quickly, full of permanents, dye jobs, body waves, shampoos and sets, trims and complicated cuts, up-dos and French twists, eyebrow waxing, French manicures, spa pedicures, gel tips, and a variety of other beautifying services. By 8:00 p.m., after sweeping up the last vestiges of hair, Liliya takes off her apron and throws it in the ham- per, full of towels and the like to be washed later on at home, along with her laundry, her sons' dirty football uni- forms, and other clothes. But first things first: As soon as she enters her home, a small ranch a few doors down from her salon, she has to get dinner started for her hun- gry, growing boys. Maybe she can catch some TV later on, Liliya thinks, as she stretches out her sore arms. Oh, but then there's the dishwasher to unload, laundry to fold and put away, and the kitchen and den to clean. Maybe she should sell the salon and retire, Liliya muses. But then where would their money come from? Sergey's business dealings are too erratic, and they're not sure that their boys can win football scholarships to pay for college. Also, her customers rely on her. They tell her often how they appreciate her 30 years of experience in hair styling, her hospitable nature, and her availability and willingness to listen to them. This and much more is why Liliya and all the other hairdressers are worthwhile persons in more ways than a million!

Did You Know?

In 1928, African-American Marjorie Joyner invented a perma- nent wave machine that curled or "permed" women's hair for a relatively lengthy period of time, allowing for longer-lasting wavy hairstyles. Joyner went on to become a prominent figure in Madame C. J. Walker's well-known hair-care company, though she never profited directly from her invention, as it became the assigned property of the Walker Company.

The Shoemaker

Faced with a mountainous pile of shoes, shoemaker Alan Friedberg turns the light on in his crowded shop in Brooklyn and begins to sort through his work. It's not even 5:00 a.m., but Alan knows he must fix many pairs of shoes before 8:00 a.m., when he opens up his shop to customers who sometimes want to pick up their footwear on their way to work. He examines a pair of tattered chestnut- brown boots, then strips off their soles, creates and applies new ones, and fixes a ripped zipper. Afterwards he gives each boot a good polish and shine.

Mrs. Gellerman with her eight kids will most likely be wait- ing outside his door at 8:15 a.m., he remembers, so he rum- mages through the mountainous pile to find the Kmart bag she dropped off last week, filled with three pairs of pumps, five pairs of loafers, and four pairs of slides. Alan proceeds to resole all of them, sew the ones with torn linings, and replace the straps on others. He sets them aside in a corner, so as not to mix them up with the many other shoes, and decides to try to reorganize his workspace.

Since his shop was broken into 10 days ago, Alan barely has had time to get it back in order. The police turned the place even more upside down than the burglars did, and they still haven't found the criminals. He now has his cousin Eli come and hang out when it gets dark, just to have someone else around to deter any hoodlums look- ing to pick on a solitary shopkeeper. Thank goodness he never keeps money onsite after hours—he was just lucky that he was not at his shop when the vandals broke in. Other than a couple of broken windows, and the theft of a piece of expensive equipment, the one that makes shoes from scratch, Alan is grateful his shop did not sustain more damage. He also thanked his wife's brother Seth for encouraging him to buy insurance to protect him from theft. Tara, Alan's wife, definitely was glad that he took Seth's advice. He could hear her now, had he not done so: "How are we supposed to pay for these repairs and feed these six children?"

As soon as his old- est child turns 10, Alan vows, he's bringing him in to learn this trade; he can't keep up with so many orders, Alan thinks, as he scratches his balding head and looks around the shop at the cubbyhole shelves he uses to organize the shoes.

Aha, there are the ones I want, hidden behind other big bags filled with shoes, Alan says to himself. Now if I can get all these other shoes put away in the cubbyholes, I'll feel much more organized, he thinks. Good thing he uses over- sized tags that can still identify which shoes belong to whom. Pushing his round-rimmed glasses up his nose, Alan focuses his pale blue eyes on the clock hanging crookedly from one of his shop's worn walls, with their gray peeling paint: 6:07 a.m. OK, if I can get this done by 7:00 a.m., he figures, I'll still have a good hour or so to finish two other orders and polish and shine the Gellerman shoes by 8:15 a.m. His head bent over and his short ruddy fingers stained with brown shoe polish, Alan deftly arranges the numerous pairs of clogs, work boots, stilettos, sandals, moccasins, wingtips, and various forms of footwear into the cubby- holes' shelves. It is this attention and efficiency that makes Alan and all the other shoemakers worthwhile persons in more ways than a million!

Did You Know?

The son of an African homemaker and a Dutch engineer, Jan Ernst Matzeliger helped revolutionize the shoe industry by developing a machine that would attach the sole to the shoe in one minute. Matzeliger's shoe-lasting machine adjusts a shoe's leather upper piece snugly over the mold, arranges the leather under the sole, and pins it in place with nails while the sole is stitched to the leather upper.

Remember also the:

- ironer
- manicurist
- seamstress
- tailor
- and all the image-enhancers!

They are each worthwhile persons in more ways than a million!

"The secret of joy in work is contained in one word—excellence. To know how to do something well is to enjoy it."

Pearl S. Buck

CHAPTER 6

Providing Nourishment

"Put your heart, mind, intellect, and soul even into your smallest acts. This is the secret of success."

Swami Sivananda

The Cook

With five minutes to go until the Friday lunchtime rush begins, cook Sunita Bevi casts her dark gray eyes around the high-tech kitchen of the midtown Manhattan restaurant that is her domain. Since she started, at the time of Umbria's grand opening six months ago, Sunita has barely had a moment to collect her thoughts. Pulling her shiny long black hair back into a tight bun and securing it with several bobby pins, Sunita wonders if the restaurant's owner, Mrs. Kalvin, has reduced the number of names on Umbria's lengthy waiting list. One day at a time, she reminds herself, as she summarily opens one of three top- of-the-line refrigerators and pulls out the defrosted chicken, veal, beef, and several kinds of fresh fish, placing them all on the long stainless steel counter that is her primary work- space. Thankfully, one of her assistants, John, has already chopped and sliced the piles of onions, peppers, mushrooms, carrots, tomatoes, and a host of other vegetables that Sunita had laid out the previous night, just before she took off her heavily stained apron and made her way home, at almost 3:00

a.m., to her cramped East Village one-bedroom apartment. Her husband was up, feeding their five- month-old, Clara, with the formula she had bought earlier that day. But the baby, reaching for Sunita, wanted her mother's milk. So, as the clock struck 4:00 a.m., the new mom started to nurse her infant.

Seven hours later, Sunita is back at Umbria. While she's grateful for a steady paycheck, especially since her husband broke his leg and was put on disability from his job at a construction company, Sunita is exhausted. She has no time to mull anything over, she tells herself as she organizes the various French cheeses and fresh breads that just arrived from the boulangerie next door. The patrons' orders start trickling in, one by one, followed by Mrs. Kalvin herself. "Sunita, I need one veal parmigiana, one gnocchi, and one chicken marsala immediately," the owner practically barks. "Those three potential investors I told you about are here, and they need their meals quickly."

"Right away," Sunita responds as she pulls the large tubs of marinara and alfredo sauce out from another refrigerator. John, taking his cue from her, turns on one of the three eight-burner, state-of-the-art stoves, and begins to take care of the four other entrée orders that had also just come in: tortellini alfredo, shrimp scampi, lobster ravioli, and mush- room risotto—not to mention three different salads. Luckily, the present patrons had not ordered any appetizers. Sunita's other assistant, Kara, called in sick this morning, so they are short-handed. Now Sunita is not sure she can leave, when her shift is supposed to end, in time to whip up a five-course dinner for her husband's parents, who are arriving today from their native India and will be staying with them for two weeks. She sighs, forcing herself to turn her attention to the tasks at hand. Within a few seconds she has deftly minced the last bunch of fresh dill, parsley, basil, and other herbs relished by Umbria's selective clientele. At any moment the 50-seat bistro will be completely full of ravenous customers. It is this precision, multi-tasking pro- fessionalism, and talent that makes Sunita and all the other cooks worthwhile persons in more ways than a million!

The Fishmonger

Long before the sun rises, fishmonger Joe Esposito has already had his second cup of coffee and finished a plate of scrambled eggs at the local diner down the street from his loft, in Manhattan's meatpacking district on the lower west side. His next stop is the Fulton Fish Market, where hordes of his fellow fishmongers scour the catches of the morning and vie for the best fish of the bunch. He sorts through salmon, lobster, sole, snapper, scallops, crabs, clams, mus- sels, shrimps, trout, tuna, tilapia, and whatever other crea- tures have been caught and brought to the bustling market.

To the eateries he supplies, Joe is simply known as "the fisherman." He is the one who stops by at 5:00 a.m. with a grin and bucketloads of fish. Joe then waits patiently for his customers to make their careful selections before continuing on to his next stop, leaving that unmistakable whiff of fish in his wake. A confirmed bachelor, Joe enjoys the rhythm of his days. Six mornings a week, in every kind of weather imaginable for the past 25 years, he has provided fish to the same 15 establishments. Some of the owners have died or moved away, but most have known him for at least two decades. Joe's easy smile, twinkling forest-green eyes, and sprightly "Good Morning" are infectious, and his customers usually invite him in for another cup of coffee and more breakfast. Occasionally Joe will interact with someone new who overly scrutinizes the quality of the fish. At times, Joe is himself not impressed with the selec- tion from which he has to choose, but he knows that din- ers depend upon his deliveries. He tries to let his customers know which fish looks better to his eye on any given day, despite the potentially higher price tag.

By the time he finishes his rounds, it's nearing noon, and Joe heads home for about six or seven hours of sleep, but not before removing his soiled waterproof pants and ther- mal tops, his waterlogged work boots, and other articles of clothing that are saturated with the smell of fish. He imme- diately dumps them into the washer that sits above the dryer in his 400-square-foot home. During the winter, the odor seems so strong to him that he also washes his lined jacket every other day, along with his gloves, hat, and scarf. Next he bathes in his narrow shower stall, scrubbing his sil- ver hair. At times, the absent-minded superintendent of his building neglects to maintain the temperature inside when it falls to below freezing outside. When that happens, Joe boils water in his microwave to use in the shower. If he does not wash his hair daily, the fishy smell will permeate indefinitely. He also never knows when one of his five brothers or sisters will drop by, with their gaggles of kids, especially since their parents passed away.

After his older sister Mara called his place a "fish hole," he tried to be more conscientious about the odor. He even bought some vanilla-scented candles from the shopkeeper next door. And maybe one day, even though he enjoys his bachelorhood, he'll meet someone friendly and mature, unlike his former fiancée. In the event that happens, Joe wants to be free of fish odors. But he is grateful to those aquatic creatures that help him make his living and fulfill his customers' needs. This enthusiasm, reliability, and integrity are what make Joe and all the other fishmongers worthwhile persons in more ways than a million!

The Supermarket Stocker

Walking back to the gigantic Costco Warehouse in Hackensack, New Jersey after her brief lunch break, supermarket stocker Ruby Timmons checks to see if there is a line at the pay phone near the entrance. She has to call her grandmother to tell her that she will be staying late. One of her co-workers did not show up, and Ruby's boss asked if she could cover for her. Ruby complied, since she could use the extra money from overtime pay. With her mom in jail and her dad nowhere to be found, Ruby has to make as much money as possible while finishing up her general equivalency diploma (GED), to take care of her little broth- er Toby and soon, she fears, her grandmother as well. It might just be a matter of time before Grandmama, as Ruby calls her, can no longer work at the Boston Chicken near their home, both of which are in Hackensack. Since Grandmama broke her hip, on the stairs leading to the base- ment in their modest ranch home, she has not been able to stand on her feet for too long.

When she receives her GED, Ruby hopes she will be able to find a better-paying job, maybe even within Costco. She feels fortunate to be able to walk to her job and receive dis- counts

48

on groceries. Stocking Costco's vast shelves for at least 60 hours a week has given her sharp bargain-finding skills. Ruby just wishes her lunch break was longer, espe- cially when she has to make a phone call and, as is the case today, there are people on line at the pay phone. She decides to try Grandmama later on in the afternoon, when she has a 10-minute break.

In the meantime, she has to finish stocking shelves on nine aisles with the bulk items that Costco's customers buy in droves: paper towels, detergent, toilet paper, shampoo, deodorant, tissues, soda, bottled water, canned soup, and mounds of other non-perishables. A few hours later, Ruby takes her break and reaches her grandmother, who in fact has just been told by the doctor that she must take a leave of absence from her own job until her hip fully heals. Ruby was afraid that this would be the doctor's diagnosis; fortunately, though, Grandmama's health insurance would still remain intact and will cover herself, Ruby, and Toby.

Ruby returns to the shelves, her slim fingers moving quickly as she places the newer products behind the slightly older ones. She calculates that she'll need another couple of hours before she can get to the produce section, where she must not only replenish all the bins but also remove the fruit—strawberries, apples, oranges, bananas, and more— that look rotten or spoiled. Thankfully, the vegetables can wait till tomorrow, Ruby's boss informed her earlier. And she must not forget about the crates of clothing that have to be displayed before the end of the week, along with all the new CDs and DVDs.

For the rest of today, though, I must focus on the top prior- ities, Ruby says to herself. If I can squeeze in two hours of studying for the GED tonight, I will be in decent shape, she thinks, as she gathers her golden brown cornrows into a scrunchie. Her eyes, the color of her hair, glaze over when she thinks of the GED exam that she'll have to take in a couple of months. But then Ruby looks at the shelves she must finish stocking and resumes her workflow, concen- trating on what she needs to do before she leaves for the night. It's this tenacity and industriousness that makes Ruby and all the other supermarket stockers worthwhile persons in more ways than a million!

Remember also the:

- coffee vendor
- fast-food order-taker
- fruit-picker
- and all those who provide nourishment!

They are each worthwhile persons in more ways than a million!

"Monotony is the law of nature.

Look at the monotonous manner in which the sun rises. The monotony of necessary occupations is exhilarating and life-giving."

Mahatma Gandhi

CHAPTER 7

For Your Health

"Keep away from people who try to belittle
your ambitions. Small people always do
that, but the really great make you feel that
you, too, can become great."

Mark Twain

The Emergency Medical Technician

With a beeping pager hooked onto her belt, emergency medical technician (EMT) Sue Nagy parks her car on the shoulder of the Harlem River Drive and, narrowing her cof- fee-colored eyes, examines her pager. It's her ambulance corps, based in lower Manhattan. They need her to come in on her day off. Pressing speed-dial on her cell phone, she calls her supervisor and learns that two of her co-workers were injured in an accident when the ambulance they were in collided with a truck. Sue's heart drops. Given how fast the ambulances need to go, she's always concerned that the vehicle's passengers themselves could wind up hurt. Luckily, her supervisor said that they were in stable condi- tion and that no patients were in the ambulance at the time. They just need more bodies to help out. Sue complies.

Before she continues to drive to work, Sue calls her husband Dave on his cell to say that she won't be able to make it to their home, the ground floor of a brownstone in Coney Island, to let out their two Labrador retrievers. Dave says he'll do his best to get home earlier, but after his dentist appointment, he also has a meeting with the mortgage bro- ker to see what they can afford if they want to buy their apartment. Thank goodness we do not have children, Sue sighs, as she edges her way back onto the highway. Our dogs are enough to take care of, she thinks, considering my random hours and Dave's. We thought we'd have more flexibility as EMTs, she reflects. That's why we got the dogs to begin with!

Traffic delays her expected arrival to the station by 20 minutes, so Sue has no time to spare. She waves to her co- workers Terri and Jack, grabs her spare uniform from the trunk of her Mazda, and races to the locker room. With Terri on her way out and only she and Jack on call, Sue needs to be ready immediately. A dispatch could come at any moment. And it does, a frantic call from Chinatown about a truck that has crashed into a restaurant full of cus- tomers. Stuffing her wavy red hair into her cap, Sue gets behind the wheel of the ambulance while Jack, a new EMT, hops in beside her, turning on the siren and lights.

As Sue speedily weaves in and out of traffic, she and Jack listen to the latest on the dispatch: "Fifteen adults, including the driver of the truck and five children are injured but do not appear critical. All persons have been vacated to a church next door. Firefighters have extracted the truck from the restaurant and neutralized it."

"Sounds like a bad one. Probably will be a long night," Sue says, just realizing that she forgot to call her parents to tell them that she would not be able to meet them at the

Hungarian Festival tonight in Central Park. They will prob- ably be upset, she reckons—Grandpa is getting an award too, as he founded the festival soon after he came to the United States from Hungary. But saving people's lives comes first, Sue reminds herself, as she pulls up outside the ruined restaurant. She and Jack run to the church, each with a stretcher and medicine bag in tow. Inside the church, the injured lie around, some bleeding, some moaning. "Let's get going here," Sue says to Jack. "Time is of the essence."

It's these life-saving efforts and preparedness that makes Sue and all the other EMTs worthwhile persons in more ways than a million!

Did You Know?

In 1893, Dr. Daniel Hale Williams, an African-American, performed the first open-heart surgery on a young man who was stabbed in the chest with a knife. By the time the injured man was transported to the hospital, he had lost a great deal of blood and had gone into shock. Dr. Williams then decided to open the man's chest and operate internally, which was virtually unheard of at that time, because any entry into a patient's chest or abdomen could easily result in infection and then death. Upon opening the man's chest, he saw the damage to the man's pericardium (the sac surrounding the heart) and sutured it. Then he applied antiseptic procedures before closing his chest. The young man survived and lived well into his 60s. While Dr. Williams is known as the first person to perform an open-heart surgery, he was also the first sur- geon to successfully open the chest cavity without the patient dying of infection. His noteworthy procedures would therefore be used as standards for future internal surgeries.

In 1940, Dr. Charles Drew, an African-American scientist, found a way to preserve and store blood, which led to his starting the world's first blood bank a year later. During his work at Columbia University, Dr. Drew found that by separating the liq- uid red blood cells from the near solid plasma and freezing the two separately, blood could be preserved and reconstituted at a later date. Dr. Drew's system for the storing of blood plasma rev- olutionized the medical profession. He also established the American Red Cross' blood bank, of which he was the first director, and he organized the world's first blood bank drive, whereby he supplied blood plasma to the British during World War II. The British military also used his process extensively dur- ing the war, establishing mobile blood banks to help treat wounded soldiers at the front lines. That same year, the American Red Cross set up blood donor stations to collect plas- ma for the U.S. armed forces.

In 1988, Dr. Patricia Bath, an ophthalmologist, became the first African-American woman doctor to receive a patent for a med- ical invention. Transforming eye surgery, Dr. Bath presented a method for removing cataract lenses using a laser device that makes the procedure more accurate. Dr. Bath's Cataract Laserphaco Probe is designed to use the power of a laser to quickly and painlessly vaporize cataracts from patients' eyes, replacing the more common method of using a grinding, drill- like device to remove the afflictions. Subsequently, Dr. Bath was able to restore sight to certain individuals who had been blind for over 30 years.

The Hospital Orderly

Pushing a meal cart, hospital orderly Mohmed Jawad jaun- tily walks down the lengthy corridor of his new employer, Columbia-Presbyterian Hospital in Manhattan. After 14 very long months, Mohmed finally found a job—and with a reputable institution, at that. How fortunate he feels! Never will he forget the emotions that unemployment pro- duced— the anxiety of when and from where he would have a steady paycheck and benefits again for himself, his wife, daughter, and son. His immediate family joined him from Egypt just three years ago, when he felt certain that his former job as a hospital orderly was secure. But cut- backs took place, and he was one of the casualties. His wife ended up finding work as a nanny, but the position didn't come with health insurance, so they were constantly afraid that one of them, especially the children, would have to go to the doctor or hospital or just need a prescription. He even considered moving them all from their one-bedroom in the Bronx back to Egypt. But just as he was about to reluctant- ly set that plan into motion, he got a call from one of the many hospitals that had received his resume.

Mohmed was nervous when he went to the interview at Columbia-Presbyterian. He had gained a substantial amount of weight when he was out of work, and he was already a bit overweight before he lost his job. He felt that his appearance would work against him. But his interviewer was a plump woman, so he began to relax as they talked about the position, specifically why he liked being a hospital orderly. Mohmed told her the truth, that he loves helping people, especially when they are sick or injured. Even though he does not have the expertise of a doctor or nurse, he enjoys making the hospitalized as comfortable as possible, whether they are lying in bed, in transit to radiology or the operating room, or about to be discharged. He likes to talk with them, tell them jokes to make them laugh, and see them smile when he brings them their food. If they need help making a phone call or turning on the TV, he is there to do so, to make their time in the hospital as pleasant as possible. As he told his interviewer, perhaps the most satisfying part of his occu- pation is transporting deliveries to patients— cards, flowers, balloons, and packages. How they light up a patient's face, and he is lucky enough to be the messenger! He believes that he has one of the best jobs around. He brings happiness with even the smallest of gestures to people who are coping with often life-threatening situations.

With a smile Mohmed greets the first patient of his 12-hour workday. "Good morning, Miss Valane!" he says jovially, making eye contact with the elderly woman. "Here are your eggs, over-easy, with bacon, whole-wheat toast, grapefruit juice, and tea. I truly hope you have a good day." Despite her delicate state (emphysema was taking its toll on her), Miss Valane beamed. This goodwill, courtesy, and respect for all humankind are what make Mohmed and all the other hospital orderlies worthwhile persons in more ways than a million!

The Social Worker

With a two-foot pile of paperwork atop her already crowd-ed desk, social worker Michiko Tawara rummages through a drawer to find a bottle of correction fluid. At the same time, she answers the phone, which has been ringing non- stop for the past three hours, ever since she walked into her windowless midtown Manhattan office at 8:00 a.m. The caller, Thomas, is one of her many alcoholic patients, and he is in the middle of a meltdown. A half hour later, while still talking with Thomas, she finally locates the cor- rection fluid she needs to fix the information she wrote on the state-funding form that must be post-marked today. She completes the form and continues to talk to Thomas while attempting to sift through 50 new e-mails that arrived in her in-box this morning. Then the other line rings. It's her 2:00 p.m. appointment, wondering if she can come in earlier, in 45 minutes. The patient says that she has to go to her chiropractor because she threw her back out, and 2:00 is the only time he has open. "That's fine, Tasha," Michiko says, as she eyes her planner with a day full of appointments and meetings. She'll just have to rearrange lunch with her mother, Michiko thinks, as she returns to her call with the distressed Thomas.

Twenty minutes later, after urging Thomas to attend his Alcoholics Anonymous meeting that evening, she proceeds to call her mother, while simultaneously delving into two boxes of folders and files that have sat next to her desk for the past three months. In order to answer one of the e-mails, she needs to find that Jacobsen file. Her mother is not happy with Michiko's cancellation. "Mom, I'm sorry," Michiko says, "but this patient is in extreme need of counseling. She's both anorexic and bulimic. She's in a very fragile state right now. At least I saw you last weekend, and I'll be coming by later this week. Plus, for me to come to Kew Gardens is inconvenient." It would help if Mom would come into Manhattan once in a while, Michiko thinks to herself.

Lines begin to form on Michiko's smooth face, as she fur- rows her brow, listening to her mother's strident voice:

"Michiko, I don't understand why you work so hard. You should find a job that pays better so you save more money. You can barely pay the mortgage each month. And how on earth are you going to find a husband when you never leave the office? When I was your age…."

"Mom," Michiko hastily interjects, "I don't work that late, I go out at night, my money is my business, and I am fine, financially and otherwise. Things are different than they were in your time. Why don't you go out with Dad to the tennis club? You always feel better after hitting some balls." And when you can focus on something other than your only child's finances and marriage prospects, Michiko wearily thinks as she feels her blood pressure rising.

Her mother's response is a dial tone. Great, Michiko mutters. She's back to hanging up on people. I think she needs some counseling herself. A knock at her door interrupts her frustrated thoughts. "Michiko," says an agitated voice. "Can I see you for a moment?" It's her boss, Kathy. "Sure, Kath. What's up?" Michiko replies.

"One of your former patients, Sheila Foster, committed an assault and battery," Kathy relays. "Her lawyer is requesting that you testify that she was emotionally distraught at the time, because her husband left her."

"Who did she attack?" Michiko asks warily, running her fin- gers through her sleek bob.

"Oh, the woman her husband left her for," Kathy says. "Sheila hit her leg with her briefcase. The woman is press- ing charges and doesn't seem intent on backing down."

"But patient confidentiality—" Michiko begins to say.

"I know," Kathy says, "but they are not looking for specifics—just a general statement. You could give it at the deposition so you won't have to go to the courthouse. It could protect Sheila from doing any jail time."

"The charges are that serious?"

"Evidently, yes." Kathy says, "Rumor has it that the woman has some connections with the prosecutor. But who knows. Just think about it. I need an answer by tomorrow morning. I've got to run."

"OK," Michiko says, sighing. "I'll think about it." But that too will have to wait, because just then the receptionist calls to let Michiko know that Tasha has arrived. Michiko makes her way to the waiting room and greets Tasha, smiling warmly. "I'm glad you could make it today, Tasha. Come right in."

It's this sincere compassion, composure under duress, and commitment that makes Michiko and all the other social workers worthwhile persons in more ways than a million!

Remember also the:

- home health aide
- lifeguard
- medical secretary
- x-ray technician and all those who work for your health!

They are each worthwhile persons in more ways than a million!

"Never work just for money or for power.

They won't save your soul or help you sleep at night."

Marian Wright Edelman

CHAPTER 8

Caring for Society's Children

**"A child's life is like a piece of paper on
which every person leaves a mark."**

Chinese proverb

The Babysitter

As the antique grandfather clock strikes 10:00 in the evening, babysitter Tanisha Phillips momentarily closes her coal-colored, doe-shaped eyes, folds her long brown arms, and breathes a sight of relief. The children in her care, six-year-old Foster and four-year-old Brittany, should be fast asleep by now, she thinks, as she rubs her head where her new auburn corn rows tug at her scalp slightly. Now she can move about freely, without worrying about waking the kids, and finish cleaning up the mess they had created. Even though she got after them to clean it up, they didn't do so to the satisfaction of their mother, Tanisha knows. So she starts to pick up the toys in the spacious great room that takes up nearly half the ground floor of the seven-bedroom villa occupied by the four O'Connell residents. Next she grabs one of the three brooms in the immense storage clos- et and sweeps the crumbs off the marble tiles in the kitchen. Then she begins to rinse off the dishes stacked in one of the kitchen's two sinks and places them in one of the deluxe oversized dishwashers.

What a day, Tanisha thinks. The bus that normally picks her up at 11:00 a.m. from her grandmother's row house in Paterson, New Jersey was running late, so she just made it in time to the O'Connell's residence in posh Upper Saddle River, New Jersey. They should be home in another couple of hours, Tanisha calculates, as she pro- ceeds to wipe down the Corian counters and shake the delicate lace tablecloth off the enormous deck that over- looks three acres of manicured gardens. She almost lets the doctor's prescription, which had become tangled in the tablecloth, fly away. That would not have been good, Tanisha mutters to herself. She wonders how she will relay to the kids' parents that Foster stuck two raisins up Brittany's nostril as Tanisha stepped away to answer the doorbell and that they had to go to the hos- pital. Luckily the neighbors, Mr. and Mrs. Mulligan, were home, and came over as soon as Tanisha hurriedly called them. After waiting nearly two hours in the emergency room, with Brittany howling while Foster alternated between comforting his sister and laughing at her— Tanisha's scolding of him seemed to do no good— the pediatrician finally saw them. He was able to remove the raisins easily enough and wrote a prescription for a mild anti-inflammatory for Brittany.

Thank goodness it's not worse, Tanisha reflects. And, thanks to the Mulligans, who gave her cab fare, she was able to get them all back to the house before dinnertime. In her rush, she had left her purse at home, but she probably would not have had enough money for the $10 ride any- way. Well, all's well that ends well, Tanisha says to herself—I'm just looking forward to crawling into my bed, probably around 1:00 a.m., at this point. This hard-working attitude, conscientiousness, and thoughtfulness are exactly why Tanisha and all the babysitters are worthwhile persons in more ways than a million!

The Elementary School Teacher

Teacher Mona Wakilu bursts into her tiny second-grade classroom at P.S. 102 in Brooklyn, her arms loaded down by a crate of books, two bags of markers and crayons, and a briefcase bursting with papers and notebooks. She sets all the items down on her Lilliputian desk and sits on her equally small desk chair, taking a moment to catch her breath as she pulls off her heavy wool coat and wet rubber boots. Why did it have to start snowing this morning, Mona wonders. If it had started last night, the kids would have not have had to come to school. Now they will be cranky that they did not get a snow day. Ah well, Mona sighs, as she puts on her comfortable navy flats. She runs a comb through her cropped black curls, her espresso-colored eyes gazing at the time—7:50 a.m.—on her silver watch, a gift from her grandfather before he died in her native Nigeria. O.K., 10 minutes until the kids start streaming in, she murmurs. She briefly looks around her classroom, to make sure that all the miniature chairs and desks are neatly arranged, that all the colorful artwork and materials adorning the con- crete walls are not falling off, and that all the lights are on and working.

Mona then begins to quickly unload her briefcase, the crate, and the bags. Next she grabs the only piece of chalk—where did the rest of the pieces disappear to?—and starts to write the day's lesson on the chalkboard. After that she runs to the heater, because the classroom's temperature is still not warm enough. After quickly adjusting the heater's ther- mostat, Mona returns to her desk to look at her planner. Oh, yes, she remembers, I have to ask Brian for the note back from his parents about setting up another parent- teacher conference.

For whatever reason, his parents never show up at these conferences. Oh, and Jamie has to bring in his doctor's notice. And Kerry and Jessica still have to bring in the permission slips for their upcoming fieldtrip to the farm in upstate New York. Twenty-five children run- ning around 16 acres of land—now that should be interest- ing, Mona thinks. Then there's the "Talent Night" that they have to start planning—no surprise that she has not had time for much of a social life of late, Mona reflects. She barely has time to see her two sisters, even though they all live together in the two-bedroom apartment they rent in Queens. When she's not grading papers at night, she's help-ing out with extracurricular activities at the school.

Such is the life of a teacher. She knows this well, given that her parents had chosen the same path. They would be happy to know that she also became a teacher, Mona reflects. Her eyes fill over as she remembers the night three years ago when she learned of their deaths in a car acci- dent. They probably would also be worrying about me not being lucky in love, she thinks, sighing. Her thoughts are interrupted by a swarm of 10 schoolchildren who sudden- ly rush into their classroom. She immediately stands up with a wide smile and greets them each by name. Right away, the minuscule classroom is full of endless chatter, shrieks of laughter, and stomps of snow-covered shoes. Five more minutes until the other 15 kids come in, and another day begins. Maybe they will have to let us out early today, Mona thinks, as she looks out the one window and sees the snow accumulating on the trees. "Ms. Wakilu, Ms. Wakilu," cry Tiffany and Patty, who slide up to her and breathlessly, almost in unison, ask, "Do you think we will go home early today?"

"We shall see," Mona replies, grinning. "Tommy, stop pok- ing Jerry. Elizabeth, let me help you take off your boots.

Children, please start taking your seats." As the students begin to follow their teacher's instructions, the rest of the class files in, and Mona starts her monologue of directions amid all the clatter and buzz of a busy city schoolroom. This care and guidance with all of children's "life's lessons" is what makes Mona and all the other elementary school teachers worthwhile persons in more ways than a million!

The Parent

Amanda Gunter, mother of three, groans as the phone rings. It's not even 9:00 a.m. on Saturday and the phone has been ringing nonstop. Now it's another telemarketer. She had hoped it would have been the contractor confirming their Monday appointment. Their small Cape Cod house in Long Island is running out of room, and they need the new addition finished as soon as possible. After declining the telemarketer's offer, she runs to use the bathroom. Washing her hands, she frowns at the unwashed flaxen curls and tired olive eyes that stare at her from the cracked mirror above the sink. She quickly dries her hands before waking up her two older children, eight-year-old Monica and five- year-old Stefan. Both have soccer games at 10:30 a.m., and they need to shower, dress, and eat their breakfast before they head out the door in less than an hour.

Just as Amanda goes to open the door to Stefan's bedroom, a wail comes from the room across the hall. It's Kyle, her one-year-old. Oh, she should have pumped last night, Amanda says to herself. She picks Kyle up and begins to nurse him as she goes back in to Stefan's room. "Honey, it's time to wake up," she gently says, placing a kiss on his cheek. Stefan turns over and accidentally hits Kyle in the face, and the baby begins to holler. "Oh, Stefan," Amanda starts to say and then stops herself.

Trying to ignore the baby's cries while rocking him, Amanda gives Stefan a hug as he rubs his eyes. "Come on, honey. You've got to get ready for your soccer game." Then she goes into Monica's room and prods her eldest to wake up. Breathing heavily, Monica doesn't answer and Amanda realizes she feels hot to the touch. Oh, no, Amanda thinks, as she feels Monica's forehead and continues to nurse Kyle. Amanda goes in the hallway and calls for her husband, "Kurt, are you back yet? I need you to take Monica's tem- perature." Amanda hears no reply but has to change Kyle before his wet diaper leaks onto her shirt.

"Stefan, please get up," she shouts as she pulls the onesie off Kyle and takes off his smelly diaper. "Oh no," she says to herself, as she realizes she's down to the last diaper. "Kurt," she yells again, "would you please come up here?" A gin- ger-haired head emerges from behind the nursery door. "You were calling me?" Kurt asks. "Yes, where were you?" Amanda replies. "Please check Monica's temperature and see if she's sick while I take care of the boys. Also, we need more diapers."

"OK, OK, I just got in—the line at the hardware store was out the door," Kurt replies. "By the way, the contractors called me on my cell, and they are coming today, at 11."

"What?!" Amanda replies. "I thought they could not come till Monday. They will make a mess with their work! Your parents and sister and family are coming over tonight at 7, and after the kids' soccer games, we have to go to the gro- cery store and clean the house before starting dinner."

"I'm sorry, hon, but we'll never get the addition done at this rate," Kurt says. Just then, Kyle throws up all over Amanda, who then hands the baby to Kurt so she can change her shirt. Just another typical Saturday, she mutters. "Stefan, please get up," she shouts at her loudest level this morning. "It's now 9:30!" This constant care and unconditional loving attention, especially during hectic times, are what make Amanda and Kurt, and all the other parents, worthwhile persons in more ways than a million!

Remember also the:

- coach
- counselor
- day care aide
- extended family
- nanny
- and all those who care for society's children!

They are each worthwhile persons in more ways than a million!

"Then seek your job with thankfulness and work till further orders,If it's only netting strawberries or killing slugs on borders;

And when your back stops aching and your hands begin to harden,

You will find yourself a partner in the Glory of the Garden."

Rudyard Kipling,

The Glory of the Garden

CHAPTER 9

Beautifying the World

The Florist

Covered with baby's breath and burgundy—and plum-colored rose petals, along with leaves the shades of autumn, florist Tyler Mavens gingerly places the remaining luscious wine-red rose in the enormous centerpiece that lies before him. "Finally," Tyler utters with a sigh of relief, as he closes his hazel eyes for a moment. He has just completed the last of 25 such arrangements for the Petruzzi wedding that is set for tomorrow in Long Island City, across the bay from his workplace, Fabulous Flowers, on Manhattan's east side. Now Tyler must clean up the leftover leaves and stems that clutter the shop's countertops before another customer arrives. Where did Anthony go, he wonders. If only his assistant could take shorter breaks. Goodness, it's already 5:00 p.m.! At least the shop is not overwhelmed with cus- tomers as much on Thursdays, Tyler muses, as he smoothes back his curly dirty-blond hair. But there is always someone who wants a special bouquet, a unique combination perhaps of lilies, gladiolas, black-eyed Susans, tulips, carnations, mums, daisies, zinnias, violets, irises, or whatever else the overcrowded shop carries, in nearly every imaginable color. The Petruzzi arrangements them- selves meant incorporating the season's newly fallen leaves, whose hues had to match the pumpkins and gourds at the shop's entranceway.

As Tyler finishes tidying up, three customers enter, each asking for two-dozen roses of varying shades, with one bouquet to include stargazer lilies and delphiniums. Oh, where is Anthony, Tyler says to himself—I'm not sure we have enough roses to last us through the day, and I need him to check our supply of them downstairs in the base- ment. But Tyler complies with an "Of course, right away" to his customers, an elderly man and two young women. As he assembles their bouquets, the phone rings on both lines. It turns out that the Petruzzi family suddenly needs four 10-foot garlands of fresh ivy and dahlias to frame the entranceway leading to their reception room. The catering hall apparently forgot to follow through with that. Tyler responds that that should not be a problem, though he knows it will be a challenge, and asks the caller—the clear- ly panicked mother of the bride—to hold for a moment as he answers the other call, all while wrapping the posies he's arranged for his unsmiling impatient customers.

As Tyler rings up each customer, he listens to the request of a new caller—the owner of the restaurant two doors down, who is best friends with Tyler's boss, the owner of Fabulous Flowers. The restaurateur is in a jam. "We're hav- ing a 70th birthday party in two-and-a-half hours, and the buds of the tiger lilies in the centerpieces that arrived are not open. The husband of the guest of honor is extremely agitated, because he says his wife will be upset if the flow- ers are not blooming, since she's a florist herself," rambles the caller in a high-pitched tone. "Do you have 100 tiger lilies with the buds open?"

Just then Anthony walks in the door, nearly colliding with the three customers clutching their floral bundles. "Anthony!" Tyler exclaims while pressing "hold" on the phone. "Please go to the basement right now and take a quick inventory. I have two urgent requests on the phone!" Right at that moment Tyler's cell phone rings. It's his girl- friend, Brenda, who wants to know when he'll be coming home, because the roof of their studio is leaking. Tyler tells her it depends on what tram he can get on to Roosevelt Island. Returning to his callers, Tyler responds smoothly: "Yes, Mrs. Petruzzi, we can create the garlands you need. They will be ready tomorrow morning, in time for your reception at 6:00 p.m." She thanks him profusely, and he has to practically cut her off to attend to the frazzled restau- rant owner on the other line. "Yes, we can replace those tiger lilies with 100 blooming ones of our own," says Tyler to him, with nary a trace of stress in his voice, though he has no idea how many such lilies are in the basement. "We'll be by in one hour." It is this supreme dependability and creativity that make Tyler and all the other florists worthwhile persons in more ways than a million!

The Organist

The choir sings a final "Halleluiah," and organist Marie Jumaneau presses down emphatically on the church organ's keys. At the First Baptist Church in Harlem, the services are almost over. Marie just has to play the closing hymn, and then she should be able to make it on time to her place of worship, the Lutheran Church in Greenwich Village. There she performs every Sunday at 10:00 a.m. Then it's off to a funeral at 1:00 p.m. and the first of two weddings else- where in the city.

Marie's schedule varies day to day, so other than her regular work at her church, she could be all over New York City any day of any week. Word has traveled about her 30 years of expertise, and she often receives referrals. In fact, late last night the First Baptist Church's pastor, who knows her minister, called her at her apartment in Chelsea to see if she could fill in for their regular organist, who had to be rushed to the hospital with a ruptured appendix. Marie was planning on having breakfast with her daugh- ter and her family, who were in town visiting from her hometown in France.

Nonetheless, she told the pastor she could make it. She needs the extra money for her retirement and wants to buy a little cottage in Provence next year. And if First Baptist asks her back again, that would be nice, too. That pastor also said he knew her late husband, so Marie thought it best to go for that reason alone, in honor of him.

At her church, the priest changes the music from week to week, so Marie never knows what to expect. Luckily she is familiar enough with the Baptist church's hymns. Usually her church's secretary, Elaine, calls her with the selections, but she had not heard from Elaine and forgot to call her because she had to take care of her sick daughter and son-in-law yesterday. Seems like the kids passed on their colds to their parents. In any event, Marie arrives to the service on time, but only to find the organ without any sheets of music. Her minister sees her and ambles over. "Marie," he says in that sermon voice of his, "Elaine is not here, and I cannot find the organ music. But you know the hymns I want to hear today: 'Eyes of our Savior,' 'Among the Fields,' 'Blessings Unto Us All,' 'Blessed are We,' and 'Come to Me, My Children.' I'm sure you'll do fine."

Marie's emerald eyes cloud over, and she smiles weakly. "Sure, Reverend," she says. How she hopes she will remember these older hymns! She walks over to the organ and massages her wrinkled hands, hoping that her arthri- tis won't kick in. Testing out the organ keys, she's relieved to find that they sound good. Untuned keys, like those that she played on at last weekend's wedding ceremony at St. Bartholomew's, can sound so dismal. After the ceremo- ny, she made a point of telling the priest that the organ needs tuning. At least the correct sheets of music were there. Perhaps her worst experience was when she had gone to a chapel to play for a wedding ceremony, and the music selections were nowhere to be found. The groom was in a tizzy—he did not want his bride to find out. Luckily, the mother of the bride remembered the songs, and they were able to find the music in one of the hymn- books kept in the pews.

If only her church had hymnbooks! Instead, the parishioners sang from handouts that only contained the words, not the music, of the hymns. I'll do my best from memory, Marie tells herself, as she puts another bobby pin in her gray hair. She strikes the C key with her right thumb and proceeds to play "Eyes of our Savior," praying that she'll remember it all. This talent and reliability is why Marie and all the other organists are worthwhile persons in more ways than a million!

The Painter

Painter Arman Harkinian directs his dark brown eyes to the blackening sky above him. It looks like rain any moment, so he makes up his mind to descend from the lad- der he's been standing on. Painting the rest of this beach bungalow's sizeable exterior will have to wait. For the past four days, he's been working at this site in Bay Head, New Jersey, and so far, the weather has been amenable. Inevitably, though, one day will be less conducive weather-wise. Arman just hopes that what he has done so far today will not be for naught; He only needs one more day of rain-free skies to finish painting the outside of the house. Carrying the can of maroon paint, he makes his way into the house, where more cans of paint, await him in the kitchen. Might as well get started on the inside, he decides, rubbing his beard, its salt-and-pepper hairs sprin- kled with specks of maroon outdoor paint.

Arman takes the stained paintbrushes out of the can, rinses them off in the nearby utility room's sink, and wraps them up in Saran Wrap to keep the bristles soft. He then washes his olive-skinned hands, tanned from hours in the sun, and proceeds to tape the edges of the cabinets that butt against the kitchen's beige walls. He has discovered that his cus- tomers feel more assured when seeing their cabinets and the like taped, and thus protected, from any potential slips of his hand, so he takes the time to accommodate them. He next lays a wide piece of vinyl on the floor, adjacent to the first wall that he selected for painting. Arman then begins to paint the kitchen's lengthy walls. He takes a small brush, dips it in the can of yellow paint, and with swift, short strokes, paints the top of the wall, where it meets the ceil- ing. With 20 years of experience behind him, he no longer needs to tape where the ceiling meets the wall; he can paint a straight line perfectly and easily.

Picking up the can of paint, whose creamy color reminds him of the butter that his grandmother used to churn in her Armenian village, Arman pours it into the slanted paint tray.

Then he takes a fresh roller out of his bag of supplies, carefully immerses it into the tray, and starts to paint the rest of the long wall. Outside, it's thundering, but Arman remains concentrated on the roller and the wall. He figures that he can finish the kitchen fairly quickly. If the rains come, he'll have time to resume painting back at his own house. That would make his wife, Georgina, happy, as he's been trying to finish painting their family room for a month now! His wife understands that the paying jobs he gets—all through good word of mouth— must take precedence.

Although their home, a modest two-bedroom in Asbury Park, New Jersey, can't come first, at least he was able to finish the nursery before Georgina gave birth to Sara just sixth months ago. Soon, Arman thinks to himself, as he begins painting the next wall, they will have to look for another house, if his mother comes to live with them and if he and Georgina have a second child. Maybe after he fin- ishes painting the family room, he can resume his hobby of painting oil-based portraits, whenever he can make the time. That's where his real painting passion lies, but ever since the baby was born, he has not had the energy, let alone the time, to devote to a canvas. Soon....

For now, Arman has this enormous beachfront house to finish. Besides the exterior, the owner mentioned painting all six bedrooms within the next couple of months. And next week he starts on a three-story townhouse that he painted some years ago. The last time, he slipped off the scaffolding and broke his leg. That prompted him to finally buy health insurance. The surgery, doctor visits, and painkillers has cost him a tremendous amount of money.

Luckily, when he and Georgina married, he was able to go on her company's plan, he thinks with relief as he spreads the velvety paint from top to bottom, left to right. Not a drop falls on the vinyl covering below his feet. It's precise- ly this professionalism and consideration that makes Arman and all house painters worthwhile persons in more ways than a million!

Did You Know?

In 1897, African-American John Lee Love received a patent for his invention of a pencil sharpener. With the portable "Love Sharpener," the pencil is put into the opening of the sharpener and rotated by hand, and the shavings stay inside the sharpener.

Two years later, another African-American, John Albert Burr, patented an improved rotary blade lawn mower. Burr designed a lawn mower with traction wheels and a rotary blade that did not become easily clogged from lawn clippings. Burr also improved the design of lawn mowers by enabling them to mow closer to building and wall edges.

Remember also the:

* choreographer
* gardener
* musician
* poet
* sculptor
* singer
* and all those who beautify the world!

They are each worthwhile persons in more ways than a million!

"We make a living by what we get, but we make a life by what we give."

Winston Churchill

CHAPTER 10

Preserving the Peace

"Be kind, for everyone you meet is fighting
a hard battle."

Plato

The Firefighter

Just as firefighter Jimmy Santos closes his weary ash-colored eyes and places his head on the narrow cot in his lower Manhattan firehouse, the sirens began to wail. He immediately jumps up and reaches for his fire-proof coat, hastily throwing it on over the rest of his uniform, one that still reeks of smoke from the office complex that was ablaze just hours before. He slides down his firehouse's pole, picks up the remainder of his gear, and joins the rest of his com- pany, who are clambering onto their fire truck.

"Where's the fire?" Jimmy asks, as the truck's red lights begin swirling.

"Over on 13th and Sixth," his Captain replies. Why does that location sound familiar, Jimmy wonders. Sixth and 13th, he says to himself, trying to jog his memory, which has been kind of foggy of late. Four major fires in two days will do that, he knows.

"Is the ARA Corporation at 13th and Sixth?" he yells above the clamor, coming to his senses.

"Yeah, apparently something in their kitchen caught on fire," the captain shouted back. "Most of the employees evacuated, but a few people are stuck there."

"Oh, no. That's where my brother's wife, Christine, works!" Jimmy exclaims. He doesn't mention that she's also pregnant. He needs to stay focused on rescuing all individuals and stabi- lizing the building. Since 9/11 and the horror that he wit- nessed and survived as he watched the Twin Towers fall, he is still having a hard time concentrating. You need to focus, he reminds himself, as he feels his head begin to throb. His brother needs his help. Maybe I should call him, Jimmy thinks fleetingly. No, that would worry him more. He decides that he'll find Christine and bring her home to the small Cape Cod house she and his brother just moved into, a few streets away from his own duplex where he lives, upstairs from his par- ents. Think good thoughts, he says to himself.

The smell of smoke reaches Jimmy's nostrils, and he turns his head up. He can see the flames clearly, as they begin to engulf what looks to be the third floor. As soon as the fire truck pulls up alongside the six-story building, Jimmy looks quickly at the evacuees congregated across the street. No Christine. "How many are missing?" he asks the police officer waiting for them.

"Looks like three men and one pregnant woman," the policewoman replies. "They are stuck in the kitchen and have been communicating via cell phone, so they are all hanging in there. But, hurry—you'll have to go up the stairs. The elevator is out of service." Wasting no time, Jimmy puts on his gas mask and rushes into the building with an extinguisher, a few of his fellow firefighters right behind him. The others douse the building's exterior with the truck's hoses and set up a safety net, in case anyone needs to jump. He reaches the third floor in a matter of seconds and surges through the office, his heart pounding. "Christine, can you hear me?" he yells, as he pulls the pin from the fire extinguisher and begins trying to put out the blaze. He can't see a thing, including his guys—the smoke is just too thick. Why isn't anyone answering, he wonders, panicking. Beams above him start to shake, and he realizes he does not have much time. Heading in the direction of the greatest heat, he nearly stumbles on four crouched bodies. He touches what looks like Christine's blond head, and her petrified eyes look up at him. "Jimmy! Thank God!"

"We have to move fast," he urges, as he instructs Christine's three co-workers to move behind him while he and the other firefighters fight the flames that have practi- cally filled the office's kitchen. As soon as Jimmy sees a window, he proceeds to open it and sticks his head out, looking for the safety net below. He spots it as his compa- ny sees him at the window. Jimmy signals them to place the net directly below him. He then guides the three business- men, who are coughing heavily, to the window, and tells them how and where they must jump. At the same time he lifts Christine, who is clutching her belly and staggering. "We're all going to get out of here fine!" he shouts to every- body. "Let's go!" And down the stairs Jimmy and Christine go, while the rest of the firefighters help the businessmen, who are about to jump into the safety net below.

Two minutes later, Jimmy and Christine are safely outside. After placing Christine on the gurney provided by the ambulance corps, who then take her to the hospital to check on her and the baby, Jimmy runs around the corner, soot flying from his normally jet-black hair. He breathes a sigh of relief upon seeing the safety net in place and learn- ing that everyone landed OK. He then stumbles to the nearest pay phone, calls his brother, and lets him know that Christine will be all right as well. It's this bravery, unselfishness, and respect for humanity that makes Jimmy and all the other firefighters worthwhile persons in more ways than a million!

The Marine

Like her father and grandfather before her, marine Heather Campion fears little. She has seen much already in her 30 years, having survived active combat in the Persian Gulf; however, as she always reminds herself, she did not experience the horrors that her father did in Vietnam or that which her grandfather did in World War II. Wherever she defends the American flag, she does so especially in their honor.

While they are proud of her fierce commitment, her father in particular had advised her against joining what has long been known as most "dynamic" force in the American armed forces, thanks to their operations by air, land, or sea. "First to fight for right and freedom, and to keep our honor clean" was a motto her father said often. His hesitance came solely from his concern that as a woman, Heather would face unfair—and immoral—obstacles in her path. Well aware of the harassment, sexual and otherwise, to which her fellow female marines are often subjected, Heather reassured her father that she could and would take care of herself. She had a black belt in karate, she remind- ed him. Nonetheless, what she did not expect was the boldness exhibited by some of the male marines—especially after one of their comrades, as recently as a week prior, had been discharged for raping a female marine. Heather, with her steely hazel eyes, only had to remind any of these lewd male counterparts of this incident, and they eventually backed off.

At times, when Heather is on base but off-duty, wearing an oversized T-shirt and a baseball hat over her cropped black hair, the marines outside of her division think of her as one of them. In the end, Heather is one of them. By the time she had finished the 13-week boot camp at Parris Island and was back home at her dad's cottage in Fair Lawn, New Jersey before heading off to Kuwait, she felt that she had earned a little respect from the mostly male recruits around her. Mastering water survival skills, marksmanship, tactics, and first aid as well as the customs, traditions, and history of the marine corps came easy to her; after all, she grew up around it. "Semper Fi"—"Always faithful"—was said as often as "How was your day?" in her parents' household. After her mother died unexpectedly when Heather was nine years old, her father played an even more active role in his only child's life. Heather honestly does not remember wanting to be anything but a marine.

Whether she's in the trenches, underwater, or high in the skies, Heather keeps the marine corps' motto at the fore- front of her mind: "honor, courage, and commitment." She knows that she must, like all marines, function as a mem- ber of a team so that they can achieve success together. When she's not in combat or training new recruits, she serves in the combat service support (CSS), a critical divi- sion of the marine corps, as those in CSS can be mobilized at any moment. Heather easily spends 12-hour days with CSS, but she always takes time to work out, at an average of two hours a day, to keep her tall, muscular frame in shape. She likes her job and wants to stay fit for it—she never knows when she may be called into combat to defend American lives, land, and liberty. Today she's at an undisclosed location, serving in the military occupational specialty designations for CSS, where she supervises construction and utilities. As a combat engineer, she ensures that bases, camps, and installations have what they need to thoroughly achieve their missions. This valor, resilience, and loyalty is precisely what makes Heather and all the other marines worthwhile persons in more ways than a million!

The Police Officer

Police officer Henry Williams crosses the street near his 13th Precinct in Manhattan and begins his daily walk. Every day he's on duty (and often when he's not), he makes a point to circle his beat's blocks, to make sure nothing is amiss. It's this community policing that has helped turn the neighborhood into an almost model area. Gone are the drug dealers and the gang members. Henry has lost track of how many he had to arrest in the past year. Feeling safe now to come out of their run-down apartments, families sit on their stoops and line the sidewalk, talking, playing, and eat- ing together. They all know Henry by name. In fact, they often ask him in for dinner, they are that grateful for a no- longer-dangerous community. Henry just smiles and declines politely—he has a job to do.

Despite the neighborhood's improvement, violent acts still take place—murders, domestic battery, and other assault cases. Just last week, Henry had to arrest a 15-year- old boy for stabbing his younger brother with a pen. Then there are the appalling child abuse cases. In all his 17 years as a cop,

Henry has never gotten past the sick feeling when he arrives at a completely disheveled home and finds an emaciated and/or beaten child—or worst of all, one who has died. It upsets his stomach so much, he wants to vomit. How could anyone do such a horrendous act? He cannot even fathom doing anything remotely like that to his two kids. Those people are so sick, he thinks. They should be locked up forever, so as not to inflict any more pain on children.

His wife always knows when he's encountered such a case. He comes home, to their two-bedroom Bay Ridge condo, in a somber mood, his tawny tiger-like eyes down- cast. But she is used to that. She knows how much pain and suffering he witnesses every day. He also still doesn't find it easy to inform a relative that their loved one has passed away, especially if the death occurred violently. Many times, when he's walking his beat, he's the first to arrive at the home of someone who has just suffered a heart attack. In that case, it's up to him to try to keep the person alive until the paramedics arrive. He has done CPR more times than he'd like to remember. At least a few peo- ple survived because of his quick reflexes and know-how. That has to be the most satisfying part of his job, Henry thinks with gratitude. That and cleaning up a neighbor- hood that deserves better, he muses, as he continues walk- ing, circumventing the two second-graders who are play- ing hopscotch in front of their home while waving to their parents, chatting across the street.

Henry is grateful to the police force for giving him this opportunity in the community. For the most part, he has been able to blend in rather well, despite some early instances of discrimination. He has come a long way from the Native American reservation, in South Dakota where he grew up. He left when he was 18 and has only gone back once, to visit his ailing grandfather. Everyone else, including his parents, had died or moved away. His grand- father almost didn't recognize him, as he had cut the raven mane that used to once flow down his back. He had just chopped off his hair for the police academy, and his grand- father at first didn't know who the close-shaven young man was. It actually took a while for Henry himself to get used to the draft he'd feel on his neck. But he got used to it, as he has gotten used to all the crime he has to curb. Just yester- day, in fact, he arrested two 20-year-olds, a man and a woman, for holding up a grocery store. Henry has learned that he can never feel too secure, no matter how welcom- ing a neighborhood may seem. It's this vigilance, caution, and caring that makes Henry and all the other police offi- cers worthwhile persons in more ways than a million!

Remember also the:

- airman and airwoman
- soldier
- corrections officer
- sailor
- security guard
- warden
- and all those who preserve the peace!

They are each worthwhile persons in more ways than a million!

"Joyful is the accumulation of good work."

Buddha

CHAPTER 11

All God's Creatures...

*"There is no greater joy nor greater reward
than to make a fundamental difference in
someone's life."*

Sister Mary Rose McGeady

The Nun

The bells of the St. Agnes Convent, where Sister Caroline Taylor has lived for the past 20 years, toll for the second time this Monday in Mahwah, New Jersey. Sister Caroline instantly stops washing the clothes from the neighboring homeless shelter and bends down to pray on the cool stone floor. She welcomes the chance to reflect and be in contact with the higher power in which she believes and trusts. She remembers the sick, the suffering, the poor, the hungry, and all those far and near, unknown and known, who are in need of guidance and faith for a better tomorrow. Then she recites the prayers that she memorized three decades ago, when she entered the convent, at barely 20 years old. A half hour later she props herself back up, massages her slightly sore back, tucks in any gray wisps of hair that may have come out of her habit, and rearranges her billowing, full- length skirts. Rubbing her ebony eyes, she resumes wash- ing the laundry.

Sister Caroline's days, as meditative as they are, are nonetheless full of activity. Three days a week she volunteers at the homeless shelter, feeding, clothing, and com- forting its inhabitants. Twice a week she leads a prayer group at the church in the neighboring town. On Wednesdays, she also visits a community women's shelter, helping the staff coordinate the myriad of details associated with assisting and counseling women and, often, children in hiding. On Sundays, Sister Caroline rises even before her usual 5:30 wake-up time. She starts her day with an espe- cially long recitation of beatitudes and prayers, resting on her knees for nearly two hours in her tiny room, furnished only with a crucifix, bed, lamp, nightstand, and closet. Then, after a bowl of oatmeal, which is her regular break- fast, she commits herself gladly to a Sunday of solitude— meditating, saying very few words, and taking long walks on the nearby nature trails. Wherever she is, she makes sure to stay within hearing distance of the bells that one of her sisters rings. (Her own days to do so are Tuesdays and Thursdays.) Then she finds as private a spot as she can find and pauses to kneel down and pray.

Working with the convent's other nuns, Sister Caroline spends the rest of her time maintaining St. Agnes and its grounds. She also organizes and attends fundraisers for the convent's chosen charities, which focus on the disabled and the tortured, both locally and globally. These fundraising events often take place on St. Agnes' lawn, and Sister Caroline coordinates with the various vendors in the com- munity—the tent supplier, the caterer, the musician, the florist, and the like—to ensure that all goes smoothly. What she finds most time-consuming is cleaning up after such an event. The guests, often well-to-do suburbanites, take little care with the convent's grounds, littering them with rem- nants of hors d'oeuvres and kicking up tufts of grass with their fine shoes. No matter what, Sister Caroline believes firmly in the causes her convent supports and will not let any inconsideration cloud her appreciation for the people who likewise support them. It is this gratitude, humility, and conviction that make Sister Caroline and all the other nuns worthwhile persons in more ways than a million!

The Pet-Shelter Caretaker

It's not even 10:00 a.m. at the local pet shelter in Port Washington, Long Island, and caretaker Sherry Givens is surrounded by eager adults and children. Entire families have come to see the puppies, kittens, and older animals that fill their crowded facility. It's Saturday, the busiest day of the week, and Sherry has been there since 6:00 a.m., tidying up the numerous kennels, sweeping, scrubbing, and sterilizing them while petting each of the 100 or so animals and feeding them. Then she takes 10 of the 50 shelter dogs out for a short walk. They all are so cute that they pull on her heartstrings. If only she could take anoth- er one home. But her parents, and two younger brothers for that matter, would not appreciate filling up their mod- est home with even more animals. They let her know that the two beagles and the Siamese cat were all they could take in. Well, she tells herself, whenever she saves up enough money to move out she'll take home more. Hopefully, she'll be able to do that soon, Sherry muses, as she refastens a barrette on her light auburn locks. She has started working at McDonald's whenever she's not at the shelter, to earn extra money.

By 9:00 a.m., after cleaning the shelter vigorously with her two co-workers, Sherry feels satisfied that the distinctive "pet odor" is gone. That should help entice prospective pet owners to take home a puppy or kitten, she thinks. Her boss would be happy about that. Just a few days earlier, their boss quietly informed them that if they could not reduce their total count to 75 animals in the next week the "surplus" would have to be put to sleep. Sherry cannot bear the thought of this prospect. Her blue-green eyes fill with tears whenever she thinks of it. So she's been calling and e- mailing everyone she knows to spread the word, and urges them to visit the shelter and consider taking home a new family member. She also places flyers in every grocery store in the area and anywhere else she thinks would help, including on telephone poles at intersections, on churches' and schools' bulletin boards, and even on the dashboards of cars parked at children's soccer games.

It seems as though her efforts have paid off. The shelter has had more visitors lately than it can remember—proba- bly close to 80 people, Sherry estimates. She moves among them, smiling and asking if they have any questions. Many do, about the animals' medical needs, paper-training, inter- acting with others, traveling possibilities, and the like. Sherry answers each and every question patiently and enthusiastically and, when possible, describes the comple- mentary services that the shelter provides, such as shots and pet-sitting. Sherry also likes to pass out free coffee and cocoa along with the chocolate chip cookies that she made the night before. She finds that these little touches often make a big difference. Anything so that no animal has to die, she says to herself when she's up past midnight bak- ing, with only five hours left to sleep before she needs to be back at the shelter. This deep-rooted kindness, determi- nation, and sincerity is what makes Sherry and all the other pet-shelter caretakers worthwhile persons in more ways than a million!

The Reverend

As the phone rings shrilly near his ear, Father Sam Parsons groggily looks at the digital clock on his nightstand: 3:00

a.m. It must be an emergency, he thinks, as he answers the phone in a clear voice. He can barely make out Mrs. Stiller's voice because she is frantic. "Father, please come to St. Vincent's Hospital. Mike and Denny have gotten into a car accident," she says, barely audible. "The doctors don't know if they are going to make it. We need your prayers."

"I'll be right there," Father Sam responds quickly, as he puts on his slacks, shirt, cardigan, socks, and shoes. He then splashes water on his face, runs a comb through what's left of his salt-and-pepper hair, hurriedly brushes his teeth, grabs his wallet and keys, and heads out the door of his one-bedroom walk-up rental in Battery Park. This is the fourth such emergency this week, and his middle-aged body is feeling it. Tomorrow, he has a funeral and a wed- ding to officiate at, and then two christenings the next day. He also has to attend the Methodist Conference in three days and catch up on the piles and piles of paperwork that have been taking over his desk and, entire office. Thank goodness for Linda, his secretary, he thinks gratefully. He does not know what he—or his parish—would do without her. The chapel itself needs so much work and maintenance that he barely has time to clean his own home. He hopes to solicit a loan at the Methodist Conference, so that they can fix the chapel's roof. If it begins to leak again this winter, that will not be good, Father Sam ruminates.

As he gets off at the subway stop located closest to St. Vincent's, his cell phone rings. It's his mother in Florida. His father is feeling chest pains, she says hysterically. They do not know what to do. Father Sam tells her to call 911 immediately and then call his sister. Why didn't they call her first, when she is in the same state, he wonders, his mind racing. "I will be on the next flight," he says comfort- ingly to his panic-stricken mother, forgetting the next day's wedding and funeral. He tries to sound strong to his mom, but inside he feels helpless and distressed. Give it all to God, he reminds himself. All will be fine, he tells himself again as he enters St. Vincent's and asks at once for the Stiller boys' whereabouts.

He finds them on the ICU floor, heavily sedated but awake. Mrs. Stiller, her eyes extremely red, rushes to him. "Oh, Father, thank goodness you are here. Only your prayers will make a difference. The doctors have operated but say the boys are both still critical," she sobs.

Father Sam takes Mrs. Stiller's hands gently and holds onto her while he places his free hand on Denny's. He begins to pray, in a low, calm tone. He continues his prayers for near- ly 25 minutes, and begins to feel the power of something greater take over. Mrs. Stiller's hands stop trembling, and she joins him in the "Our Father" prayer. Their united voic- es fill the hospital room and bring a sense of serenity to it, for those few moments. Than Father Sam shuts his tired blue- gray eyes tight and beseeches God to spare the boys' lives. It is this unswerving devotion, steadfastness, and faith that makes Father Sam and all the other reverends worth- while persons in more ways than a million!

Remember also the:
• animal rescue officer
• horse handler
• imam
• monk
• rabbi
• zookeeper
• and all those who tend to God's creatures!
They are each worthwhile persons in more ways than a million!

"Blessed is he who has found
his work. Let him ask no other
blessedness."

Thomas Carlyle

> "Always bear in mind that your own
> resolution to succeed is more important than
> any other thing."
>
> Abraham Lincoln

A Little "Thanks" Will Go a Long Way...

In this book I have attempted to profile the individuals who enhance our everyday lives. These are people who work "behind the scenes," even though we generally see them in plain sight every day. Truth be told, they are everywhere. Next time you are out and about, really look around you. You may be surprised at all the different kinds of work being performed to keep our cities and towns, and our lives, operating smoothly!

In addition to those occupations I described, there are many others that deserve attention. Consider the supermarket cashier who, day in, day out, scans and rings up all the items we purchase. Or the doorman, who meets and greets visitors and residents, continuously opening and closing doors, taking packages, providing security. Or the waiter, waitress, or busboy who serve us and clean up after us, for minimal wages and tips. Then there is the postal worker who delivers our mail in all kinds of weather. What about the newspaper reporter—another kind of worker we take for granted? Without their hard work and dedication, our newspapers would be nothing but blank pages! Or picture the factory worker bent over an assembly line for eight hours or more each day, to make the things we need.

These are each hard-working individuals who form the infrastructure of society. How can we not notice them and appreciate their value? And if we are one of them, how can we not value ourselves?

Last but in no way least, when we reach our final day on earth, there is the undertaker, the person who endeavors to make a painful time a little less difficult. And, at the very last moment, many of us are beholden to yet another member of society, the gravedigger. Neither gardener nor farmer, this laborer digs the land to perform another important function.

Hopefully you now understand why I wrote this book: to show how every living human being provides a valuable service to the world at large. Rich or poor, celebrated or unknown, beyond considerations of race, color, education, and other superficial factors, and whether we contribute to the broad mosaic of life on planet Earth as a neurosurgeon or as a pest control technician, we are, each of us, a worth- while person in more ways than a million!

Simeon W. Johnson
Brooklyn, New York

ABOUT THE AUTHOR

Prolific author Simeon W. Johnson is a successful entrepreneur with a book and gift boutique: swjenterprises.com. A former radio and television electronics technician, Mr. Johnson has worked as a welder, a shipbuilder, and a housing inspector. He received a master's certification in radio and TV electronics  from National Technical Schools, Los Angeles, CA. He also earned his FCC First Class General Radio and Telephone License, with a specialization in radar applications. Born in Jamaica, West Indies, Simeon is the youngest son of 13 children, with nine brothers and three sisters. Mr. Johnson came to the United States in 1967 and is now a proud U.S. citizen.

His books, which are sold on his website and on amazon.com and barnesandnoble.com, are: *A Myopic Life Resonated from the Brink of the Abyss; Romw vs. Ramb Reveals God, Adam and Creation;* and *An Unforgettable Tribute to Our Heroes and Victims of 9/11.*

Often in demand as an inspirational speaker, Mr. Johnson has been a guest on numerous radio and television talk shows including: XM Satellite Radio, Washington, D.C.; KQDJ Radio, Nevada; Cool 107, Michigan; WCKX Radio, Ohio; WMCA 570AM, New York; WRVC AM930, West Virginia;

It's Your Turn Show, Pennsylvania; WAD Radio, Vermont; KLSB Radio, Virginia; WPTA Radio 930 AM, New York/New Jersey; and many others.

For Simeon Johnson, **You're a Worthwhile Person in More Ways Than a Million!** is the book closest to his heart, since it powerfully celebrates the value of each human being. This book, along with his previous successes, he believes, offer tangible verification of how anyone can make a difference in this world, no matter how overwhelming the odds may seem when that individual sets out on his or her unique journey in this adventure we call life.

Mr. Johnson now lives in Stockbridge, Georgia. He is a devoted father to Cheryl and Cassandra and has a grandson, Brian and granddaughters, Amira, Gabriella, and Simone.

Available at amazon.com

&

barnesandnoble.com

Lightning Source UK Ltd.
Milton Keynes UK
UKHW010726250520
363803UK00002B/276